LIBRARY MANUALS

Volume 3

FUNDAMENTALS OF LIBRARIANSHIP

FUNDAMENTALS OF LIBRARIANSHIP

An Introduction for the Use of Candidates Preparing for the Entrance Examination of the Library Association

DUNCAN GRAY

LONDON AND NEW YORK

First published in 1949 by George Allen & Unwin Ltd

This edition first published in 2022
by Routledge
4 Park Square, Milton Park, Abingdon, Oxon OX14 4RN

and by Routledge
605 Third Avenue, New York, NY 10017

Routledge is an imprint of the Taylor & Francis Group, an informa business

Copyright © 1949 by Taylor & Francis.

All rights reserved. No part of this book may be reprinted or reproduced or utilised in any form or by any electronic, mechanical, or other means, now known or hereafter invented, including photocopying and recording, or in any information storage or retrieval system, without permission in writing from the publishers.

Trademark notice: Product or corporate names may be trademarks or registered trademarks, and are used only for identification and explanation without intent to infringe.

British Library Cataloguing in Publication Data
A catalogue record for this book is available from the British Library

ISBN: 978-1-03-213109-2 (Set)
ISBN: 978-1-00-322771-7 (Set) (ebk)
ISBN: 978-1-03-213249-5 (Volume 3) (hbk)
ISBN: 978-1-03-213252-5 (Volume 3) (pbk)
ISBN: 978-1-00-322832-5 (Volume 3) (ebk)

DOI: 10.4324/9781003228325

Publisher's Note
The publisher has gone to great lengths to ensure the quality of this reprint but points out that some imperfections in the original copies may be apparent.

Disclaimer
The publisher has made every effort to trace copyright holders and would welcome correspondence from those they have been unable to trace.

FUNDAMENTALS OF LIBRARIANSHIP

An Introduction for the Use
of Candidates preparing for the
Entrance Examination
of the Library Association

by

DUNCAN GRAY
F. L. A.

LONDON
GEORGE ALLEN & UNWIN LTD
RUSKIN HOUSE MUSEUM STREET

FIRST PUBLISHED IN 1949

This book is copyright

No portion of it may be reproduced by any process without written permission. Inquiries should be addressed to the publishers

PRINTED IN GREAT BRITAIN
in 11pt. Baskerville type
BY BRADFORD & DICKENS
LONDON, W.C. 1

GENERAL INTRODUCTION

In the general introduction to the earlier volumes in this series, the original editor, Mr. W. E. Doubleday, wrote:

"This new series of Handbooks is intended to supplement the larger Manuals issued by Messrs. Allen & Unwin and the Library Association. . . . (It) is issued independently by Messrs. Allen & Unwin, and the range is sufficiently wide to make the volumes appeal to administrators, librarians, assistants, and students who intend to sit at the professional examinations."

Though the main features in the practice of librarianship are not subject to any great change, many of the details of library administration are under a constant process of development which seeks improvement, e.g. of methods of cataloguing, of book classification, of shelf arrangement, and of service to readers. Those may best be dealt with in small monographs which may be revised at sufficiently frequent intervals.

There is a special need for up-to-date material for the use of candidates preparing for Library Association examinations, either by private study, correspondence course, or, more fortunately for them, at one of the full-time schools of librarianship, and it is hoped that this series will prove particularly helpful to them. It is hoped also that the volumes will be found useful to practising librarians, particularly to those engaged in special departments, or in reorganisation, or revision of library systems which have become out of date.

CONTENTS

I.	By Way of Introduction	page 9
II.	The Practice of Librarianship	19
III.	The Library Committee	27
IV.	Public Library Systems of Great Britain	37
V.	Library Finance	47
VI.	The Library Departments	54
VII.	Bookstock: 1. Selection, Accessioning and Processing	68
VIII.	Bookstock: 2. Classification	78
IX.	Bookstock: 3. Cataloguing	87
X.	Bookstock: 4. Care of Stock, Revision, Stocktaking	97
XI.	Bookbinding	106
XII.	Membership and Registration	115
XIII.	Bye-laws and Regulations	124
XIV.	Issue Methods	131
XV.	Reference Libraries: Material and Method	141
XVI.	Co-operation—Regional and National	151
XVII.	Reports and Statistics	161
XVIII.	Publicity	171
XIX.	The Library Association	180
	Index	185

CHAPTER I

BY WAY OF INTRODUCTION

LIBRARIANSHIP does not call for the precision of a machine, carrying out the same operation with monotonous repetition and identity; but it does call for order and system, for without these in library work there cannot be efficiency. This is true of all types of library from the largest national library to the smallest special or village library; and it is the reason for the close attention that beginners must give to the learning of the routine details of their everyday work. A misplaced book or file or record means loss of time and efficiency when that book or file or record is required; and sometimes, as in the case of a misplaced file in a special library of a research department, it may mean the holding up of work of many people, with all the irritation and expense this entails. So, though routine duties are not by any means the end and aim of librarianship, they are so important to smooth working that efficient routine work is rightly insisted on.

Though routine details are not the same in all libraries, they are designed in all cases to provide the same or similar results. They concern, first of all, the stock—and in this collective term are included books, prints, maps, manuscripts, serials, periodicals, separates, pamphlets, broadsides, lantern slides, microfilms, gramophone records and any other items any library collects and preserves for the use of its clients. The most important part of the stock is likely to be the books; but this is not necessarily always so, as in special libraries connected with manufacturing works or research stations the work carried out is ahead of published books, and the important stock may be items from scientific periodicals in a variety of languages, or abstracts of these, or even manuscript reports. Whatever the stock may be, however, it must be arranged in the library in the settled order prescribed for it when it is not in use. One of the first tasks for any new worker in a library is to learn the system of arranging stock, which usually means learning the outline of the classification scheme in use. Most public libraries use the Decimal Classification invented by the American librarian, Melvil Dewey, and first published in very simple form in 1876, since when it has been revised and enlarged through fourteen editions to become the monstrous volume it is in its latest form. Other libraries use other classification schemes such as that of the American Library of Congress; or an expansion of the Dewey classification system made by the Institut International de Bibliographie and called the *Classification Décimale,* or Dewey Extended; or the Subject Classification invented by the English librarian, James Duff Brown; or the Colon Class system invented by an Indian librarian, Ranganathan. The main principle of all of these systems is to divide knowledge as contained in books, or written down, into a series of main divisions which do not overlap at any point, and then to divide each of the main divisions or classes into subclasses in greater and greater detail. Classification is a subject of major importance to librarians, and one to which special attention must be given.

As will be found, it is an essential part of a scheme for classifying books that each subject is represented by a symbol or mark, a shorthand version of the name of the subject, and a knowledge of these symbols or marks grows with practice. They are used whatever the nature of the material to be arranged may be, whether books on bookshelves, prints or broadsheets in boxes, or papers or separates in vertical files.

The first duties of the new librarian are likely to be very much concerned with the details of shelf arrangement. A library exists for the benefit of its users, and during any working day many items are borrowed and many others returned. Those borrowed have first to be found, and herein lies the need for exact work in shelving and filing; and those returned have to be replaced in their shelf or file position. According to the type of library, and the number of daily transactions, the amount of work of this kind varies. In a busy home reading department of a public library there may be as many as 10,000 transactions in a single day; in a research library of a firm of manufacturers there may be as many as 1,000 or as few as half a dozen. In this connection a point of great importance to the librarian and his work is whether users of the library have personal access to the material or not. If they have, and this is the usual arrangement in the home reading departments of public libraries, there is likely to be much displacement of books on the shelves, as the person untrained in library method is notoriously careless in this respect. This means that there must be a shelfcheck each day to correct these displacements, as well as the routine duty of returning used books to their proper places on the shelves. The work is comparatively simple, particularly after the main outline of the classification scheme in use has been mastered; and it is apt to become monotonous and tedious, a condition which invites careless work. It is an essential of good library practice that this work should be well done, for reasons already touched upon; and an interest may be well sustained in those concerned if they make a practice of visiting other libraries whenever possible, and of examining the shelves of those other libraries in order to compare work in them with work in their own library.

There is a benefit to be obtained by the young librarian in doing this routine shelf work which is not sought for and is, in fact, what chemists would call a by-product. It is that in looking at the same or similar books day after day, the descriptive details of these books become fixed in the memory. If the library is well stocked and carefully selected, it should contain the best books available, and the titles and authors' names become well known to the librarian. If he carries this a step further, and takes the trouble to examine the contents of a few of them each week, he will do two things—first, he will increase his personal knowledge; secondly, he will become more efficient in carrying out his duties, as he will become more and more able to help readers who ask questions about the books they require.

This shelf routine work is not only important to the library but equally important to the librarian. The more he examines books both in his own and in other libraries, or in bookshops or private houses, or wherever he may come into contact with them, the more he will build up that book knowledge, and that sense of discrimination which comes from it, which are the hall-mark of the good librarian.

The second part of routine work which is likely to engage the attention of the young librarian is the catalogue, and a library without a good catalogue is deficient in its services, as it will be asked questions which may be within its scope to which it cannot provide a satisfactory answer. Those who do crossword puzzles find that there is often an interchange of the words 'catalogue' and 'list' which supposes them to be synonyms—but they are not. A catalogue, it is true, lists the contents of the library, but it does more than this, and it is not so much a list as a series of lists which are inter-related to each other; in short a 'list' is simple; a 'catalogue' is complex. A library catalogue is designed to answer any one of four main questions which may be put to it.

(1) Does the library contain a certain book of which author and title are known?
(2) Does the library contain a book of which only the title is known?
(3) Has the library any books by a named author?
(4) What books does the library contain on a given subject?

The library catalogue should be able to answer all these questions with the possible exception of number 2.

In order to answer these questions the catalogue is usually divided into two parts, one of them arranged in order of subjects, and the other in alphabetical order of authors' names, and sometimes with titles of books intermingled and arranged in alphabetical order of the first word of the title other than the definite or indefinite article. The part arranged in subject order uses for this the symbols for the names of subjects taken from the system of classification used by the library—the Decimal, the Subject, the Library of Congress, or other. These symbols are usually numerals or letters or a combination of the two, and the entries are consequently arranged numerically, or alphabetically and then numerically. A key to these symbols is essential, and this is provided by having an alphabetical index of subject names, each followed by the classification symbol for that subject.

If an answer is required for the first need given above —Does the library contain a book by a given author with a known title?—this is quickly obtained by referring to the author catalogue. If only the title of a book is known, the author catalogue, if it contains title entries, should supply the information, but it is not usual for a catalogue to contain all titles of novels, and it may be necessary, therefore, to consult one or other of certain works of reference which should be available, and of which details will be given in a later chapter. The third question—What books does the library contain by a named author?—is also answered by a simple reference to the author catalogue. The fourth question is more difficult—What books does the library contain on a given subject?—as this means using the subject or classified catalogue. To do this, the first approach is to the alphabetical index to the classification scheme, which, as indicated, should be available for use with the subject catalogue, and it is necessary to do this carefully. Not only must one look at the subject name as given, but also if necessary, under any alternative names or synonyms; and one must remember also that whereas some books deal only with one subject, others deal with two or more, and particulars of these more complex books must be given as well as of those which deal with but one subject, and that clearly. At the beginning of the study of librarianship it is sufficient to appreciate that this is a subject of great complexity and difficulty.

calling for wide knowledge of books, of books about books, and of sources of information for its proper performance; but the questions that beginners will be called upon to answer will usually be of the kind that can be answered by the intelligent use of the subject catalogue and the alphabetical index to it. If a dictionary catalogue is provided, this combines all entries in one alphabet.

Again, as with books, library workers should take every available opportunity of examining catalogues other than those of the library in which they work. In some they will find that much greater detail is given than in others, e.g. the catalogue of a large reference library will give not only the essential particulars of a book—author's name, title, number of edition, date of publication, and particulars of illustrations—but also size in inches or centimetres, number of pages and whether consecutive numbering or not, place of publication and name of publisher, and possibly a note about the book, or details of its contents. It is a good plan to know the exact and correct cataloguing details of one or two books of first importance that should be in all general libraries, and to check the entries for these books in any catalogue examined. This is not, of course, an infallible guide to the quality of cataloguing in the library concerned, but it is often an indication that can be checked with others.

The important thing to remember about catalogues and schemes of book classification is that they are not ends in themselves, but means to an end. That end is the provision of facilities for the rapid and intelligent use of the library, and it is only in so far as they fulfil this essential condition that they are worth the great labour entailed in using them. It has been said that the aim of librarianship is to bring order out of chaos, and it is only by this that the details of librarianship can be evaluated. These are in the third part of routine duties—those concerned with the relations between members of the staff and those who use the library. It is usual to refer to those who use libraries as 'borrowers,' though 'readers' is perhaps a better term. Their relations with the staff vary according to the type and size of the library. In the British Museum, for example, there is a wide selection of books available for use on open shelves. For the use of the remainder it is necessary to know the authors of required works, as the British Museum catalogue is an author catalogue only.[1] Works of reference are provided for the use of readers to enable them to find authors' names, however, and there is always a librarian on duty at an enquiries desk, who will give any assistance that may be required. Books are applied for on paper slips which are ruled to give spaces for catalogue details and the numbered desk of the reader, and messengers bring the books to that desk. This, with slight variation, is the method of most large reference libraries.

In university libraries the method is similar, but most books may be borrowed by students and taken away from the library for stated periods during term time. Sometimes, in addition to the main university library, there are also college libraries, or faculty libraries which may or may not be under the direction of the university librarian. University libraries are used mainly by members of the university—undergraduates, post-

---

[1] There are subject indexes to the additions made to the British Museum Library from 1880. Supplements are now published at five-yearly intervals.

graduate students and members of the staff—who should know what they want, and it is a common thing for library method to be explained to new students by the university librarian at the beginning of each session.

In special libraries there is close association between the librarian and the members of the staff who use the collections. The number of persons using a special library may be very few; the contents are likely to be highly specialised, and the services the librarian is called on to perform are of equally high specialisation.

Public libraries deal with greater numbers of readers than any other type of library. The numbers are, indeed, so great, that the staff-reader association is developed on lines which aim at combining high speed of operations with complete accuracy. In most cases association is limited to the charging out of books borrowed, and their discharging on being returned, and in many libraries, the staff is so limited in numbers that little more than this perfunctory service is possible. This may be true equally as much for the small county library village centre as for the central lending library of a large city with its possible 5,000 books borrowed on a single day, which may mean twice that number of separate transactions. Methods of mechanising this work are now being tested, which may lead to a saving of staff time which could very well be used for other purposes. These other purposes are the very desirable ones of providing more and better individual service in the choice of books than has hitherto been found possible in more than the smallest proportion of libraries. It is a service which has been developed much more widely in America than in England, where it is known as the readers' adviser service.

The routine work of libraries, as the beginner finds, is divided, then, into the three broad divisions of stock and shelf arrangement, the provision of guides to the collections, and the staff-reader association. It varies much in quantity and in kind according to the type of library, and no librarian should remain satisfied with a knowledge of his own department or library. He should take every opportunity of widening his knowledge by observing the working of other departments and other libraries whenever he can.

CHAPTER II

THE PRACTICE OF LIBRARIANSHIP

At first glance there appears to be little, if anything, in common between, for example, the village centre of a county library and the central library of a large city. In the one there is a small collection of perhaps 250 books, possibly set out in bookcases, possibly only spread out on tables or benches because bookcases are not available, with a voluntary worker in charge to issue the books to the handful of people who attend on the one night a week the centre is open to the public; in the other there is an imposing building near the centre of the city, housing a series of co-ordinated departments, each in charge of a qualified librarian, with a considerable bookstock, a staff of assistants, some expert, some clerical, some trainees, the co-ordination and direction of the whole being carried out by a chief officer of the city corporation. Little in common, indeed, at first glance, but each is doing essentially the same work, that is, providing for the reading needs of the local population. These reading needs are sometimes simple, sometimes complex; they may appear settled in grooves, but the grooves are shallow, and not necessarily permanent. The essential function of libraries is to provide for the book needs of those who use them, and the function of librarianship is, on the one hand, to make all necessary arrangements, and to carry out all processes which will bring the reader and the book he requires together and, on the other hand, to take all necessary steps to conserve the books, to ensure that they are used properly and not kept beyond the time allowed for loans by the library regulations. A further duty of an essential nature which is special though not exactly exclusive to public and county libraries, is to make the stock known to readers by a variety of publicity and display methods which are described in a later chapter.

The national, special and university libraries are used for the most part by those who know exactly what they want, and are conversant with library method from the standpoint of the user of libraries: which is to say that they are familiar with library catalogues and their methods of preparation, and with author and subject bibliographies. The public and county libraries have many users who are equally conversant with library method; but the majority of those who use them are not so, and their reading tastes are often of a most elementary kind. Without help or stimulus from the library they are likely to remain with restricted and narrow powers of book selection. It is in the field which this state of affairs creates that libraries and librarians can do most useful work in broadening the outlook of the average man and woman, in bringing new and unknown interests forward, and in pursuing that course of informal suggestion which is their privilege and the part they have long played in the provision of facilities for further education. It has been well said, in recent reports dealing with the need for fuller development of schemes for further education, that much good work has been done in the past by agencies not directly or professedly educational, of which public libraries are an important member.

The use made of public libraries divides broadly into

three main streams—first, education; secondly, culture and information; and thirdly, recreation. The terms do not exclude each other: what is educational for one may be culture for another or even recreation for a third; but the broad division of the bookstock of public libraries into the two groupings of fiction and non-fiction is the usual way of separating recreation from the other purposes of book reading. It is not a satisfactory separation, as there is probably much more to be gained by the reading of the works of famous authors of past days such as Scott, Dickens, George Eliot, Jane Austen, Wells, Kipling, Galsworthy or, of our own day, such as Charles Morgan, E. M. Forster, J. L. Hodson and D. L. Murray, than many of the volumes of highly coloured and often inaccurate biographies which rank as non-fiction. The test of reading is its effect on the mind, and the reading of books which add to the sum of our knowledge, help us to understand the working of the mind—our own and others—and assist us in developing our powers of reasoning and our sense of discrimination, can have nothing but good effect, and is not to be belittled by the patronising manner in which the reading of 'novels,' grouped as a *genre* and with no distinction between the good and the bad, is sometimes treated. The reading of the great novels of English literature has its place in the educating of the human mind just as firmly established as the reading of history or philosophy, to which subjects, and many others, it can add its quota of commentary.

In subjects which are educational from the standpoint of school and college—the arts and the sciences which make up the vast accumulation of knowledge as contained in books—the public library has much to offer.

A main function of the science of librarianship is the selection of books, and it is the duty of the librarian to take each subject in turn, find out what books are available in each of these subjects, and from personal examination of the books themselves, and a careful study of those books-about-books called bibliographies, by discussions with experts, by consulting the reading lists compiled on these subjects by acknowledged authorities on them, by considering the expressed needs of readers, and by examining the stock of other libraries, to determine which books are likely to be of greatest service to his own library and his own town or county. It is work that calls for close study and persistent care; it must be done for each class of book in turn; and then it must be the subject of frequent revision so that the inaccurate, the misleading or the out-of-date may be removed and its place taken by new acquisitions. Part of this revision is brought about by the weekly examination of notices of new publications—book reviews in literary and scientific periodicals, publishers' catalogues and announcements, book lists compiled for circulation by the National Book League, and by other libraries; part of it, particularly in the home reading departments of libraries, is done by a shelf check which never ends, proceeding from class to class in turn. Only in this way, and by this constant attention to bookstock, can the work of any library be made fully effective; and in the case of books on scientific and technical subjects its importance cannot be too greatly emphasised, as new discoveries, new inventions, the perfecting of new processes and the constant changes that are so marked a feature of our mechanical age supersede the processes and supplement the theories of the textbooks, which may become only too quickly misleading or inaccurate or incomplete. An example of this is to be found in the recent development in architecture and building of the unit system and the processes incidental to prefabrication. The world shortage of materials, once profuse, necessitates the use of new materials, which in turn call for new or adapted processes, and this gives the name by which the unit system is sometimes called, namely 'the adaptive.'

There is not the same need for constant and wary supervision of stock in other main divisions of knowledge. Philosophy and psychology do not change as subjects, and though modern philosophers and psychologists publish their new or modified theories of the working of the human mind, these supplement but do not supplant the writings of the earlier philosophers. Common law does not change, though statute law may and does. The classical writers of the ages remain a bulwark against change in a changing world; a play of Shakespeare's may be easier to read in a modern edition than in the first folio edition, but its sense and content are in no way changed, and its message is the same for us who read it now as it was for those who heard it at the 'Globe' some 350 years ago.

Revision, pruning, substitution, supplanting of bookstock, all have their place in the science of librarianship, and there can be no end to these processes in a library for home reading; but certain works no longer desirable as guides must be preserved for reference or for historical purposes, and the librarian in his daily work must take account of this also, that he may conserve when he should. There is an essential difference in the service performed by placing books on open shelves where they are available to all, and supplying to a reader a particular book or edition of a book asked for by him. Even here, though, the safeguard should be adopted of pasting a note in out-of-date books describing their inaccuracies or shortcomings.

Librarianship as a science and as a profession is designed, among other things, to methodise the selection and display of books, and to give guidance in choice where this is desired. It is in methods of display, the provision of reading lists, and personal guidance that librarianship gives its best service as an agency for the education and culture of the mind, and though the terms 'education' and 'culture' are as unpopular with men and women to-day as the mutual improvement societies so respected a generation or two ago, they are just as much needed and wanted as ever they were. But the average approach to them is a personal one, and nothing is likely to cause greater embarrassment to the librarian than the proffering of unwanted help. At the same time it must be realised that access to the shelves of a library with anything from 10,000 to 50,000 volumes from which to choose is not an unmixed blessing to the average reader, and though the classified order of the books on the shelves is completely intelligible to the librarian, it may be nothing more than mumbo-jumbo to the would-be reader. This is the reason for the popularity of the 'returned books' shelves, on which are placed books as they are returned to the library after being borrowed for home reading. Many readers do not move far away from these shelves, their argument being that if someone else has found a book worth taking home, it may suit them equally well. Two methods are in use to overcome this difficulty. The first is to have small displays of books, each display dealing with a subject, a country, or an author, and arranged alongside a poster or pictorial background which describes the display. This often leads a reader to an interest in an unknown and hitherto untried field. The second is to have an enquiries desk, with an invitation to readers to ask for what help they may require; and in the hands of a well qualified and sympathetic librarian the work done from a desk of this kind can rapidly develop into an important feature of the service.

The use of libraries for recreation is literally enormous. There are millions of people who obtain their most satisfying relaxation through reading, mainly the reading of novels, biography and books of travel, though not confined to these classes of books. The provision of a constant diet of detective stories or westerns or love stories may be considered as a service hardly requiring a local government department to be responsible for it. But two important points must be borne in mind when this matter is under consideration. The first is that the level of mental attainment varies considerably in adults as in children, and what is the lightest effort for one person may be an exercise of much effort to another, and to concentrate the attention of the mind over a period of hours in the reading of a book, however light in tone, if this is the limit of understanding, must be beneficial. The other point is that many readers, after a period of serious study, enjoy very greatly the relaxation of reading a piece of fiction of a chosen type.

These are some of the important details of the practice of librarianship. There are others that may involve media other than books; but the main features of librarianship are those which concern the reader-book relationship in all its many ranges, and at all of its many levels. Librarianship is not something which can be learnt in a course of study and then be considered a finished product, capable of all calls that may be made on it. It is rather the learning of a method of working, which requires constant exercise to keep it in fit condition and able to meet the calls of many varied kinds that are made upon it in day-to-day work. And this day-to-day work may be in a large city library, or a branch library of town or county, or a village centre. The large city library will have the material within its own walls to meet most if not all of the calls made on it; the branch of a town has the central library to which it can refer what is beyond its scope; the county branch library of whatever size, from the regional branch to the smallest village centre, has the resources in material and expert staff of the county library headquarters, to which it can refer what is beyond its scope.

General resources do not end even here, as all libraries, great and small, lie within the working of the Regional Library Bureaux (described in a later chapter) which, briefly, are organised to arrange loans from library to library, and, in effect, bring within the reach of all users of libraries a bookstock running into millions of volumes.

CHAPTER III

THE LIBRARY COMMITTEE

THE library committee and the source from which comes the money to pay for the service are always closely associated. For the National Libraries—the British Museum and others—the source is the national exchequer, and the committee of management, or Board of Trustees as it is called, is appointed by a Minister or a Department of State. For university libraries, the library committee is a committee of the council of the university. For special libraries there may be a committee of the governing body, such as the Council of the Library Association, which has a house and library committee or, in the case of a special library of a business firm, the supervision may be allocated to an officer of the company such as the Chief of the Research Department.

In the case of public libraries, town and county, the governing body is known as the Library Authority, the name given in Acts of Parliament dealing with public libraries. For counties and the county libraries, the Library Authority is the county council. For towns it is the local council, or corporation as it may be called if the town is also a county borough, or a city which has received a grant of incorporation; and the local council may be a county borough council, a borough council or an urban district council. The powers possessed by towns are identical, whatever the status of the town may be, with the exception that some towns have additional special rights or privileges which come from the terms of special local Acts of Parliament, and apply to these towns only.

Most, though not all, local authorities—that is county councils, county borough, borough and urban district councils—having many kinds of responsibilities and activities, carry out their duties through a system of committees. Each department of work, or group of departments, is directed by a committee appointed by the authority for that purpose. In counties the library committee must be the education committee, or one of its sub-committees, as this is laid down as an obligation on county councils by the Public Libraries Act of 1919, the first and only general Act which deals with county libraries in England and Wales. In towns the committee is usually appointed for the one purpose of managing the library or libraries, and is called the Public Libraries Committee; but sometimes the work is joined to other local authority work such as the management of museums, and its name is extended to include this additional function. Occasionally the duties of the committee are wider still, including, for example, the management of art galleries or public parks. In practice, it is better to have a committee with a single broad function, as otherwise a tendency may develop to give preferential treatment to one of the committee's functions at the expense of the others.

There is a clause in the 1919 Public Libraries Act which allows borough councils or urban district councils (but not county borough councils) to refer their powers under the Public Libraries Acts to their education committee, and in one or two cases, e.g. the Borough of East Ham, this has been done. It is not a power likely to be exercised much in the future, since the Education Act of 1944 has terminated the existence of all education committees of local authorities other than those of county councils and county boroughs.

The powers of local authorities to establish public libraries are contained in Acts of Parliament. For England and Wales the main statutes are those of 1892 and 1919; for Scotland they are the Public Libraries Acts of 1887 and 1920 for towns, or burghs as they are usually called, and the 1918 Scottish Education Act for Scottish County Libraries; for Northern Ireland they are the Irish Public Libraries Act of 1855 and the Public Libraries (Northern Ireland) Act of 1924, as amended in 1947. These Acts of Parliament set out in precise terms exactly what may be done, what cost can be incurred, what may be provided, and how the work is to be governed. All the Acts withhold from any public library committee which a local authority may appoint the power to raise a rate or to borrow money, which powers are rigidly reserved to the local authority itself. All public library Acts are 'permissive'; that is to say, it is not obligatory that local authorities shall establish public libraries. The library committee, then, is a subcommittee of the education committee for all county libraries; it may be the education committee for towns of lower status than county boroughs; for all other towns it is a standing committee of the authority (i.e. a committee which goes on from year to year, in contrast to a special committee which comes to an end when the work it has been appointed to do has been completed), with functions that deal either with libraries only, or with libraries and other affairs such as museums, art galleries or parks. It is the usual procedure for local authorities to appoint all their standing committees at the first meeting following the annual election of councillors, one-third of whom must retire each year, either to be re-elected or supplanted, and the business of electing committees usually follows the election of the Mayor (or Lord Mayor) or Chairman of the Council.

At the time of electing the standing committees the local authority sets out what are to be the powers and duties of each of the committees and, according to the Acts of Parliament, or statutes as they are usually called, which set out the powers of the local authority for each of its functions, the authority states which of its powers, if any, it delegates to the committee. Sometimes, for public library work, the local authority delegates all of its powers—with the exception, of course, of those relating to raising a rate or borrowing money—sometimes some, rarely none.

In the case of county libraries, referred by statute to the education committee, that committee may appoint a sub-committee to deal with the county library only, or it may place the library work under one of its existing sub-committees, such as that for higher education, or for further education, in which case the sub-committee concerned may decide to deal directly with library affairs, or appoint a committee to deal with them which, as a sub-committee of a sub-committee, would be referred to as a minor sub-committee. Education committees must, by statute, consist partly of members of the local authority (councillors) and partly of persons who are not members of the local authority, referred to as co-opted members. These co-opted members of committees have full rights of debate and of voting on the committees of which they are members, but no power of any kind on the local authority itself. They are usually chosen because they have special knowledge of the subject of education (or, in the case of other committees, of the subject matter of such committees); for example, if there is a university or university college in the area of the education committee it is usual to appoint the vice-chancellor or principal to membership.

Local authorities must appoint co-opted members on certain committees, and they have the power of appointing them on others, e.g. the library committee. In the case of public libraries, there is much to be said in favour of co-option of specialists to assist in book selection, a main function of library organisation, where their advice and expert help can be of great value. The disadvantage of appointing them is that they have neither voice nor vote in the deliberations of the local authority itself which, for most public libraries, is the last word in all its important affairs. There is no generally accepted view on this matter. Many public library committees have co-opted members, many have not.

The work of the library committee divides into three broad groups of type of business. The first is concerned with matters over which the committee has had full powers delegated to it by the local authority. These are usually concerned with the essential details of management—the approval of book purchases; the passing of accounts for these and for all the ordinary necessaries such as fuel, cleaning materials, stationery and office equipment; membership and use of the libraries; the holding of lectures and exhibitions; relations with other organisations such as (in towns) the education committee, the community centres, the rural community association, drama societies, literary societies, and others. These matters will probably, either monthly or from time to time, be the subject of report to the council.

The second type of committee business is that which is within the scope of the year's work, for which the necessary funds are available in the budget for that year, but not within the powers delegated to the committee by the council. Such matters usually relate to all separate items costing £50 or more, and may include painting and decorating of buildings, purchase of items of furniture, the carrying out of structural alterations to buildings, the appointment of senior members of the staff and, generally speaking, matters of a special kind, outside general routine business. These are carefully considered by the committee, along with any necessary competitive estimates of cost received from firms of contractors. In the case of painting and decoration, alterations to structures and matters of a similar nature, these will have been surveyed by the engineer or architect of the authority, who will have prepared the details in the form of a specification for the use of firms of contractors, on which they can base their offers (or tenders) for carrying out the work. It is the usual practice for tenders for the carrying out of such work to be submitted unopened to the committee concerned, and to be opened and listed at a meeting of the committee. The committee then consider the details and, unless there is some very good reason against it, the practice is to accept the lowest price or tender which has been submitted. As the power to accept or reject is usually retained by the council, the committee cannot finally accept, but makes a recommendation embodying its views, which will be put to the council at its next meeting. This type of business is referred to as 'matters requiring confirmation by the Authority.'

The third type of business relates to new work not within the scope either of the powers delegated to the committee or of the budget of estimated expenditure of the year's work. It may be concerned with a proposal to carry out a plan of reorganisation, or the setting up of a new service, or the purchase of a site for a proposed new branch library. Matters of this kind are usually the subject of a special report from the committee to the council, and if they are likely to involve expenditure in the current year they will also be the subject of an application to the finance committee for a supplementary estimate.

Towards the end of each financial year, the committee prepares its estimate or budget of proposed expenditure for the financial year next following, a subject to be considered in greater detail in a later chapter. This estimate of expenditure goes from the library committee to the finance committee, who review the estimates of all committees and, either with or without alteration, submit the details and totals of all the committee estimates to the council for approval. This is the necessary step that must be taken before the amount to be collected from all ratepayers can be assessed, and the details in each list of committee headings must not be varied in any way without the express sanction of the finance committee, and possibly of the council.

Procedure in committee work is carried out under a well-tried system. The clerk or secretary (for town library committees usually the town clerk; for county libraries the director of education) summons the meetings usually on a settled and regular day at a settled and regular time. Sometimes the summons is special; but with local authorities regular meetings are fixed for a year ahead and entered in an official diary which is circulated to all members of the authority, who are expected to attend the meetings of the committees of which they are members as noted in the diary. As a reminder, and to give notice of any alterations or additional meetings, it is a common practice for town and county clerks to send each week a card in the form of a calendar for the following week, with all committee meetings noted on it, to all members of the authority. In addition to this, some clerks send out to members of committees an agenda paper of the business to be done at each meeting, which members are expected to bring to the meetings. Sometimes this is not done, but the agenda papers are placed on the committee room table immediately before the meeting takes place. A chairman is appointed at the first meeting of each new committee after the annual elections of councillors, and he presides at all meetings if he is present. Some committees also appoint a vice-chairman who presides in the absence of the chairman. If neither chairman nor vice-chairman is present the members attending the meeting appoint one of themselves to act as chairman for that meeting only. The town clerk (or director of education, as the case may be) or his representative attends to take notes (minutes) of the proceedings.

Business is dealt with in orderly fashion, item by item, as given on the agenda paper, invariably the first item being the reading of the minutes of the last meeting which, if they are approved, are signed as correct by the chairman and become a record which may not be questioned. The second usual item is to deal with matters arising out of the minutes. Other items include the approval of accounts for purchases during the previous month, the submission of the departmental report of the chief officer—for public libraries the chief librarian or the county librarian—the list of required items to be purchased for which sanction is needed; and then follow the non-routine items such as special purchases, staff appointments, recommendations as to new fields of work, and so on. The clerk to the committee takes notes of all matters for minuting purposes, and of committee decisions which are made by the voting of the members present, a show of hands and count being taken whenever necessary. When the committee is equally divided on any special item, the same number of members voting for and against it, the chairman has a casting vote to decide the issue. If he decides not to use this vote, the particular item is 'not carried,' and therefore is not proceeded with.

There is no essential difference in procedure of library committees whether they are standing committees of a town council, or sub-committees of the education committees, as in counties. Matters decided by the committees which require confirmation go, in towns, to the town council, and in counties to the county education committee. In the case of county education committees, there are certain powers which the county council may not have delegated, and these will require the additional confirmation of the county council.

Twice at least during each year the work of the public library, whether of town or county, comes to the notice of the local authority. The first is when the annual budgets are submitted, to which reference has already been made; the second is when the annual report of the library committee is submitted. The annual report is an important document, as it relates, in narrative and statistical form, the details of the work of the libraries during the past year, and it is often used to tell not only what has been done, but also what remains to be done. Some library committees do not submit an annual report, but their organisation is the poorer for its absence.

In county library organisation, because of the wide area covered, it is sometimes the practice to appoint local committees to supervise the work of branch or regional libraries of the county library. This is a good method of developing and keeping a keenness of local interest in the working of the branch. Local committees are appointed by the county library committee, who specify carefully which powers are to be exercised locally and which are to be referred for consideration to the county library committee. It is the usual practice for the county librarian to attend or to be represented at meetings of local library committees.

There may be special variations in procedure in different places, but in the main, library committee work proceeds in the manner described.

CHAPTER IV

PUBLIC LIBRARY SYSTEMS OF GREAT BRITAIN

MUCH has been written about the public libraries of Great Britain since Edward Edwards' pioneer work, *Memoirs of Libraries*, was published in two volumes in 1859—a work much used by writers of the earlier textbooks of librarianship. The Library Association has published many works since its foundation in 1877; and other important source-books include the annual and special reports of the Carnegie United Kingdom Trust; the Report of the Departmental Committee on Public Libraries of 1927; the Library Association Survey of Public Libraries of 1938; and the McColvin report of 1942. They tell a story of great progress in developing an idea; but they emphasise that progress has been very uneven in its distribution.

The first Public Libraries Act was passed in the year 1850, this applying to England and Wales only. The first Scottish and Irish Act was passed in 1853. The Act of 1850 encountered much opposition in its passage through Parliament, one objection being that the spread of popular education would be harmful to the well-being of the country, as it would have an unsettling effect on the labouring classes, who might be tempted to think that Jack was as good as his master; and another that, as some of the speakers against the Bill had, so they said, neither need nor use for books, these were quite unnecessary, and the provision of public libraries would be a waste of public money. No attempt was made to make the Acts compulsory. Their adoption, and the spending of public money in providing local library services, was left to the wish and will of local residents; and the early Acts stipulated that a local poll of ratepayers must be taken to ascertain the majority opinion. Another curb was that the amount that might be spent by any local authority on this work was limited—at first to $\frac{1}{2}$d. in the £, and later to 1d. in the £ of rateable value.

The first public libraries Acts were passed before the statutes which created county councils (1889) and made the education of all boys and girls compulsory (1870). The idea behind the agitation for public libraries was the need to provide reading matter for those who could not afford to buy books themselves, a need which had already been demonstrated by the opening in many towns of artizans' libraries and mechanics' institutes, which provided the use of books and newspapers for members at a small charge; but, successful though these were, they were insufficient to meet the ever increasing demand for books.

The first Act limited expenditure to $\frac{1}{2}$d. in the £ of rateable value, and did not allow any part of this to be spent on the purchase of books which, it was supposed, would be forthcoming from wellwishers of the movement. This proved to be an error of judgment, and later Acts amended conditions to allow books to be purchased, and increased the rate limit to 1d. in the £. The unit for adoption of the Acts, until 1919, continued to be the parish or the town (borough or urban district).

Local adoption of the Public Libraries Acts and the establishment of libraries did not proceed at anything like the speed which had been anticipated by the leaders of the movement. By the year 1869 the number of adoptions was only forty-six; but from that date onward there was a much increased rate of progress, due to a variety of causes. First, there was the putting into operation of the Education Act of 1870, the first compulsory Education Act to operate in England and Wales; secondly, there was the founding of the Library Association seven years later, and the publicity for library affairs which this brought and has sustained; thirdly, but not until the last decade of the nineteenth century, there was the series of benefactions from Andrew Carnegie, the Scottish-American millionaire, whose gifts to numerous towns for the erection of public library buildings has made the term 'Carnegie Library' a commonplace; and fourthly, there has been continuance of the work begun by Andrew Carnegie by a Trust, founded and financed by him, called the Carnegie United Kingdom Trust, which established experimental county libraries during the period 1915-18, thus giving impetus to the need for a new Public Libraries Act to enable county councils to become library authorities. The new Act was required also to meet the equally great need for removing the rate limitation of expenditure on libraries. Of these two needs it is hard to say which was the greater, for, without new legislation, the development of the county library movement, begun so promisingly on Carnegie Trust money, was completely blocked; and the 1914-18 war had so reduced the spending value of money that the fixed income, in all but a very small number of established public libraries, was quite inadequate even to carry on the existing service, and any extension—and at that time great extensions in public education were much in favour—was out of the question.

The coming into operation of the 1919 Act was an event of the greatest possible importance to public libraries in England and Wales. Immediate needs requiring additional income, due to the fall in the purchase value of the pound, were able to be financed, and new or held-up projects became possible of accomplishment. Movement in every direction has taken place since that year, and it is true to say that for book supply, staff conditions and general service matters there have been improvements on an extensive scale in many libraries, though, unfortunately, not in all of them. Improvement has not been accomplished everywhere, due to the still-operating permissive nature of public library legislation. It is still purely a local matter what shall be spent on the public library service, and though there are many excellent services, there are also many which are wretched; and for this reason there is a strongly held opinion that library legislation should be made compulsory, and that, among other things, a system of government grants should be instituted to operate in similar manner to those for public education, so that local incomes may be augmented and possibly levelled up. This would mean the institution also of supervision by government inspectors of libraries, and the probable imposition of minimum standards of provision of services. The standards would not be likely to help the better library authorities; but they would be of immeasurable advantage to many backward areas, and they would be likely to lead to a much needed amalgamation of library areas.

The removal of the rate limit was confined to the public libraries of England and Wales, town and county. The Scottish amending Act of 1920 did not remove the limit, but fixed a new limit of 3d. in the £ for town (burgh) libraries in Scotland. The Northern Ireland Act kept the limit at one penny, with extension possible to the maximum of threepence at the discretion of the responsible department of the government, but the rate limit was entirely removed by a Statutory Order in 1947. County libraries in Scotland are governed by a clause in the Scottish Education Act of 1920, and no limit on expenditure is imposed. There is, therefore, the unfortunate position in Scotland that whereas the county libraries can be extended indefinitely at the discretion of the local education authority, the town public libraries are limited in what they may do; and, in addition, Scottish burghs must pay both burgh and county library rates, which is known in Scotland as double-rating, and is extremely unpopular.

The present state of public library legislation is most unsatisfactory. Greater powers are needed everywhere, and for Scotland there should be financial provision equal to that which England and Wales enjoy. The removal of the rate limitation in Northern Ireland should be followed by similar legislation for Scotland. Even then, the position in Scotland and Ireland will be no more satisfactory than it is in England and Wales now. There will still remain the need for government grants, and the consequent imposition of minimum standards of library provision.

Surveys of public library provision in the United Kingdom have been made at intervals since a pioneer work of this kind was prepared by Professor W. G. S. Adams for the Carnegie Trust in 1915. Among other things, this survey by Professor Adams revealed that the rural areas were almost entirely without library provision, which led to the experimental schemes for county areas financed by the Trust, and in turn to the phenomenal development of the county library movement which has taken place during the past thirty years. The Adams survey revealed also the great unevenness of town services.

A further survey was carried out by the Secretary of the Carnegie Trust, Colonel J. M. Mitchell, which was published in 1924, and showed such improvements as had followed the removal of the rate limitation in 1919, but also showed continued unevenness of development. But by this time, a major activity of the Library Association was exercising a considerable influence on public library affairs. This was the work of the Association in carrying out professional education of librarians. Education of librarians was initiated by the Library Association in the nineties, but for the first twenty years it was very limited in scope. Professional advancement did not at that time depend entirely on the possession of Library Association certificates; but from about 1910 they began to feature in advertisements for posts in libraries, and this increased, showing those who were keen on advancement that, if they would progress, they must qualify. That professional education had a demonstrable practical value soon became evident to those authorities employing both qualified and unqualified assistants; and it became still more evident when qualified librarians were appointed to reorganize libraries previously administered on makeshift lines. The results obtained after systematic reorganization were often spectacular to a degree, and this process has now been carried out so frequently that it is too well known to need particularization. There still remain in local authority circles those who doubt the value of professional training in librarianship, but they are, happily, a small and decreasing number; and the weekly advertisements for librarians which specify as obligatory the qualifications granted by the Library Association are a cumulative answer to their doubts.

The Carnegie Trust Report of 1924 and the activities of the Library Association led to the appointment, in the same year, by the President of the Board of Education (Mr. C. P. Trevelyan), of a Departmental Committee "to enquire into the adequacy of the library provision already made under the Public Libraries Acts, and the means of extending and completing such provision throughout England and Wales, regard being had to the relation of the libraries conducted under those Acts to other public libraries and to the general system of education." The Report of this Committee was published in 1927, and it stressed the need for bringing a public library service to those towns and villages still without it. It also stressed the need for better reference library facilities, and a much greater measure of co-operation between libraries, including interlending of books. The main effects of this report were the creation of the union catalogue of the Metropolitan public libraries—later to lead to a system of interlending of books and interchangeability of readers' tickets—and the development, through the Central Library for Students (now the National Central Library) of the regional library bureaux, also concerned with the interlending of books. The continued effect of these movements has been to bring within the reach of the member of any co-operating library a book stock numbering several millions.

The Library Association Survey of 1937 was financed by the Rockefeller Trust, and was a personal survey in the nature of field work by a corps of experienced librarians, who described their visits to libraries and their interviews with librarians throughout the United Kingdom and abroad. The sum of their contribution is the same as that obtained from the questionnaires sent out by the Carnegie Trust and the Departmental Committee; and exactly the same conclusions are to be drawn: much progress in some libraries, particularly since 1920; complete stagnation in others, and no minimum standard of efficiency in being or in prospect.

During the early part of the second world war the Library Association Council, through its Emergency Committee, decided to consider possible post-war developments, and to obtain material for this purpose, the Honorary Secretary, Mr. L. R. McColvin, made a series of visits to libraries throughout the kingdom. Following this, he prepared a detailed report, which described the public library service as he saw it, and made many suggestions for alterations. Two main suggestions were first, that the existing areas of administration—the town and the county—should be discarded, and their place be taken by a series of regional 'units,' with, so far as possible, a minimum population of a quarter of a million; and secondly, that regional reference libraries, financed by the government and not locally, should be established to bring good reference library facilities within the reach of all. There were many other suggestions, and the McColvin Report is a document which must be studied in detail by all serious students of librarianship.

The Library Association published its own proposals

for post-war development, which were debated and amended at the Annual Conference of the Association in 1946.

The position at the time of writing (mid 1947) is that suggestions to change the present areas of administration are not favoured; but there is a widespread feeling that necessary developments are retarded by the unsatisfactory financial position of many public libraries. It has been suggested in the Library Association proposals that

(a) public library provision should be made compulsory;

(b) there should be government grants, and all public library services should be under government supervision;

(c) any necessary changes in library areas should be made.

As public library services are in being for practically the whole of the kingdom already, there cannot be any great measure of disapproval of the first of these suggestions. The second suggestion is very widely approved and, having regard to the great diversity in rateable values between the poorest and the richest town or county, financial adjustment, and in many cases help, is essential if any development is to take place. Development would almost certainly call for careful consideration of the present library areas, and there can be no doubt that many existing areas are too small to provide an adequate service, and should be attached to a larger unit.

What is without question is that there is much too great a gulf between the good and the bad libraries, and progress demands that a minimum standard should be instituted and enforced. It is a bad thing for the country as a whole that facilities for education and mental culture and recreation should vary in efficiency to the extent they do at the present time.

CHAPTER V

LIBRARY FINANCE

In library administration, money is required for four purposes: first, for the buying of books and other library stock, and for their binding and general upkeep; secondly, for the payment of staff wages and salaries; thirdly, for building upkeep, including cleaning and repairs; and fourthly, for administration and equipment costs. Capital expenditure, which includes the purchase of building sites and the building and furnishing of new libraries, is not usually considered in discussing departmental finance, as such expenditure is non-recurring and, as a rule, governed by special decisions and procedure. For the large expenditure on new buildings it is customary for local authorities to borrow the necessary money, and repay the loan by a series of annual payments, including principal and interest, over a period of years.

The annual expenditure is forecast in what is referred to as the annual estimates or budget. The procedure to be described here is that used by local authorities for their public libraries, town or county; but some similar method is essential for all institutional or special libraries if they are to be properly administered and to keep abreast of the times.

The method of preparing annual library estimates is to have a list of headings which, taken together, cover all the library requirements which cost money. Sometimes there is a very extensive list of headings; sometimes similar needs or purposes are grouped under broader terms—these are matters which are settled locally. A workable series of headings is as follows:

1	Books / Periodicals / Binding of books	Books
2	Salaries and wages / National insurance / Superannuation / Uniforms	Staff
3	Rent, rates and insurance / Lighting and heating / Furniture, fittings and repairs / Cleaning materials / Painting and decorating	Upkeep of buildings
4	Printing and stationery / Postage and transport charges / Telephone / Travelling expenses	Administration charges and equipment

In addition to these items, many libraries have a regular heading for repayment of loans; and some include a heading for small items of miscellaneous expenditure, e.g. subscriptions to societies, or purchase of plants and flowers, though it is better to do without the term 'miscellaneous,' as it is usually possible to fit such things as may be included there under one or other of the main headings.

The determining of the amounts to be placed under the different headings calls for much thought and calculation. Insufficient income means inadequate service, but, on the other hand, extravagance in estimating is likely to lead to trouble for the person who has framed the estimates. They are the subject of very critical scrutiny first by the library committee, then by the finance committee, and finally by the full council; and the treasurer of the Authority will consider it part of his duty to point out any great variation in the same item in different years, which, in due course, the estimating officer—usually the chief librarian—will be called upon to explain.

There is only one proper method of preparing estimates, which is to take each of the items in the budget, work out the forecasted details for the coming year of what is covered by the item, and put down the figure arrived at. All these details or working papers must be carefully preserved so that they can be referred to during the period of preparation and submission of estimates, until finally these are approved by the council. It is wise to keep them even longer, for at least the year to which they apply, in case of requirements for adjustment or reduction, or for any other matter relating to them which may arise.

Many attempts have been made to produce an accepted system of standards on which estimating may be based. There is little or no difficulty about the group numbered three above—upkeep of buildings—with the exception of the item relating to painting and decorating. At the time of writing (1947), there is considerable difficulty in obtaining materials and labour for painting and decorating of public buildings; but normally it should be done at intervals not exceeding five years. If buildings require painting and decorating, it is a wise plan to seek the advice of the surveyor's or architect's department in fixing the figure to be submitted for this work. It is also a good practice to have the library building or buildings surveyed each year in order to ascertain the nature and extent of any repairs likely to become necessary—pointing of brickwork, repairs to roofs, renewal of drainpipes or of floorboards, for example—and to include an expert's estimate of cost for such things.

Administration and equipment requirements do not vary greatly from year to year, though at the present time costs of paper, strawboard, binder's cloth, and indeed most items of equipment, are constantly rising, and this, though it is a symptom of the unsettled state of postwar affairs, and will not continue indefinitely, must be taken account of at the present time.

The main difficulties of library estimating are concerned with the purchase and replenishment of the bookstock and the payments for staff. These are of first importance and are controversial, as there is no settled standard for either. They are of first importance because a weak bookstock cannot meet the calls likely to be made on it; and even a good bookstock will not be used to its best advantage if the staff is weak either in numbers or quality.

With regard to bookstock, there are certain minimum requirements for any library: a special library must be able to answer specialist calls made on it; a university library must satisfy the teaching requirements of the different faculties; a public library must have an adequate stock capable of meeting all ordinary requirements, but bearing in mind that special needs can be met through the use of the regional library bureaux and by interlending generally.[1] For a new library, a workable

[1] It should be emphasised that interlending ought to be confined to scarce and specialised works. In the day-to-day work of the regional bureaux many applications are received for books which are neither scarce nor specialised.

minimum stock figure is obtained by taking the possible membership of 25 per cent of the total population to be served, and multiplying this by three. This is a minimum figure on which to work, and extension of stock in future years should increase it by at least one-third. After that, local circumstances will decide what is best; but the additions of new stock year by year should equal or exceed withdrawals and losses. The cost of books is undergoing change for a variety of reasons, and at present is a rough average of three books to the £. To arrive at the basic cost per volume for estimating new needs, the total of last year's book accounts should be divided by the number of books bought.

In discussions on library book funds, it is a common practice to try to standardise in terms of cost per head of population, and twenty years ago, an analysis of book costs of well-stocked and much-used libraries gave an approximate figure of fourpence per head of population. At that time, much library stock was bought in the secondhand book market, the secondhand shops were very well stocked, and books were plentiful. The position is greatly changed to-day, as the secondhand book market is by no means what it was; and, in consequence, it has become the general practice of libraries to buy the major part of their books in new condition. This has had two effects: it has saved much staff time in searching for cheap copies of books required; and, as a result of buying new books, the costs to libraries have much increased. Prices of secondhand books have also increased, sometimes considerably. Various estimates of book cost per head of population are now put forward, varying from ninepence to half-a-crown; but a better method is to survey actual needs by actual costs, and determine the figure required in this way.

Estimating for wages and salaries of staff has been helped by the introduction of the national grading scheme for local government officers, and the adoption by all local authorities of this scheme, and the various joint industrial councils' wages schemes. The latter are accepted as pronounced locally. The former are more difficult, as local authorities have not adopted a uniform system of interpreting the national grading scheme. The Library Association has circulated its views as to grades which should be allotted to different library posts. These are on the high side—rightly so—and have not yet been generally adopted, but some authorities have adopted them, and others will follow in due time.

The crux of this matter is the number of persons required to staff a library adequately, and their grading into the general and professional divisions. Practice varies considerably. The relevant factors for calculating staff requirements are either work done as measured by book-issues, or total population. The minimum requirement of a library, however small, is a staff of three. Beyond this, a minimum staff is one for every 50,000 of book issues per year or per 5,000 of population. The ratio of professionally graded staff to general division staff should be approximately one to three.

Of the estimated yearly cost of a public library upwards of 90 per cent comes from rates, and the remainder from library income—fines for overdue books; sale of waste paper, etc. Receipts are given by the library for all money received, and this is paid into the treasurer's department at regular intervals. The major part of the income is from the payment of fines, and their frequent occurrence makes it desirable to have the quickest possible form of giving receipts. Written receipts should be avoided because of the time taken in producing them, and a common practice is to have tear-off printed receipts, each roll carrying a running number, so that a day's takings may be calculated by ascertaining the number of receipts used. A better system (adopted in some libraries) which avoids the use of rolls of differing values—½d., 1d., 2d., etc.—is the use of a cash register which throws out a ticket of the amount stamped on the machine, and at the same time records this in a roll inside the register. The requirements are speed and accuracy. All other money received needs a written receipt in a miscellaneous receipts book which takes carbon copies.

For public libraries the book-keeping is done by the authority's treasurer and accountant; but it is a good thing for the librarian to keep his own check of expenditure month by month under each of the headings in the year's tabulation of estimates, so that he can space his expenditure evenly over the year's work. This does not apply to items relating to repairs or painting, or purchase of furniture and fittings; but it does to the working details such as purchase of books, stationery, cleaning materials and, generally speaking, stock and administration details.

CHAPTER VI

THE LIBRARY DEPARTMENTS

A SMALL library may carry out the whole of its work in one public room. A large library may have a dozen or more separate departments, each with its own room or rooms, librarian and staff, e.g.:

1. Reference Library.
2. Lending (Home Reading) Library.
3. Children's (or Young People's) Library.
4. School Libraries Department.
5. Commercial and Technical Library.
6. Music and Drama Library.
7. Visual Aids Department.
8. Cataloguing Department.
9. Branch Libraries Department.
10. Further Education Department.
11. Administration Department.
12. Photographic Department.
13. Stores Department.
14. Publicity Department.
15. Bindery.

Medium-sized libraries may carry on most of these activities in some convenient system of grouping. The first seven of the departments listed are used by the public—the remainder mainly by staff only. For the departments used by the public there are certain details of great importance to successful administration; but there are no hard and fast rules, and in practice there is very considerable variety. A tendency in modern planning has been to increase the space occupied by public rooms and to decrease the height of shelving; but, as regards size, this tendency is not confined to recent buildings, as some built thirty or forty years ago with Carnegie money are, and always have been, too large and pretentious.

The ideal to be aimed at is to provide accommodation which is functional, or entirely suited to its use—rooms large enough to avoid overcrowding at the busiest periods; furniture and fittings which are of good material and workmanship, and are also designed in good taste and capable to their use. These are the important considerations, and attempts to impose 'standards' of planning or fitting are to be resisted. For a long time, standardisation was imposed in public libraries by the Cotgreave indicator, a device to regulate borrowing of books and to keep records of all borrowings, when readers did not have access to the bookstock. A later standardisation, still much used, is the 'sheep pen' form of entrance and exit to libraries, and a radial arrangement of standard bookcases, in order to achieve complete oversight of readers from a central point—the staff counter or 'enclosure.' There is little to be said in favour of standardisation in planning and furnishing libraries, and much to be said against it. At the same time, however, there are certain important principles which it is wise to follow: they are the result of experience and experiment, and are of general application.

First of all, as to size of room, it is desirable that a room to which the public are admitted freely, and where any number over twenty persons may be in the room at any one time, should not be smaller than 1,200 to 1,600 square feet in area—that is, 30' × 40' or 40' × 40'. To have this floor area in one room is better than having greater floor area in several separate rooms. If the library is for a small local population, up to, say, 5,000—e.g. a town or county branch library—it may be found best to carry out all the library services in the one room, devoting one corner to books of reference, another to books for children, and putting any periodicals or newspapers provided for readers on tables placed centrally. A good town branch of this type—in a prefabricated building—may be seen at Lincoln; a good county branch at Bakewell, in Derbyshire.

Single-room libraries such as these contain the essential services of a public library, and departmentalisation starts from this point. As will be seen, there are four main services: the home-reading service, the reference service, the reading-room service, and the young people's service; and there are many varieties of grouping of these according partly to the size of the place and the numbers of persons making use of the services, and partly to the nature of local library buildings. As size of local population grows, and with it the numbers making use of the service grow also, the local demands increase in extent and kind, and the requirements of each of the services for its satisfactory performance tend to become specialised. With this comes the necessity for dividing the work into departments. At first, these are the well-known departments of the medium-sized public library, namely, lending library, reference library, reading room and junior library—the latter a development in many places of the past twenty-five years. As size and numbers grow again, it becomes necessary to divide the departments, so the reference library gains a sub-department for commerce, or for commerce and technology, and another for photographic reproduction. The lending library spreads over into branch libraries, as one central building is not able to carry the whole of the work of the town; and as the branch libraries' work needs to be co-ordinated with the central library and each with the others, a branch libraries department becomes necessary. Following this, as it is most desirable to have a single method of cataloguing and classifying for the system as a whole, it is advisable to centralise the work into a cataloguing department. This process of budding-off sections may lead to division of work into as many as fifteen departments for the largest library systems. Smaller ones will develop their own system of grouping of the essential four types of services. The main requirement of each of the fifteen departments listed above are as follows:

1. *Reference Library.* Being a place for private study, a reference library must be quiet, must provide a good stock of works of reference, and facilities for using them in reasonable comfort. The size of the bookstock and of the accommodation provided varies according to the size of the library and the number of readers making use of the service.

It is neither possible nor desirable to state minimum reference library requirements, as so much depends on local circumstances. A reference library provided on a new housing estate may not be used at all at first, and may take years to establish itself: but it is, none the less, an essential further education facility which should be available to all; and as a contrast, the reference library of a small town with a historic past may be in constant and considerable use.

Essential bookstock includes what are usually termed 'ready-reference' books—local directories, and yearbooks such as *Whitaker's Almanack,* the *Post Office Guide,* and *Who's Who*; next, there should be composite works, e.g. encyclopædias such as the Britannica and Chambers's; language dictionaries, to explain the meanings of English words and to give equivalent words in other languages such as French, German and Russian. There should also be comprehensive works on separate subjects, such as Bryan's *Dictionary of Painters and Engravers,* Hastings' *Dictionary of the Bible,* the *Dictionary, of National Biography* and the *Oxford Companion* volumes; and a representative selection of books relating to the locality—its history, topography, genealogy and industries. With these as a basic stock, and wherever possible on open shelves and available to all without form-filling or any other barrier, much can be accomplished.

It is a usual practice to make the non-fiction stock of the lending library available for use in the reference library. For this purpose it is necessary to have a copy of the catalogue of the lending library available, and also a supply of application forms ruled to take particulars of author, title and call number of books required, and name and address of reader. This is the method used also for obtaining reference library books not on open shelves, which, in the larger reference libraries, form the bulk of the stock.

There are many kinds of readers' desks (or tables) and chairs in use in reference libraries. Where space allows this, the best practice is to have a separate small table for each reader—size not less than 2′ 6″ × 1′ 6″. Where separate tables are not possible, this is the minimum space that should be allotted to each reader. Chairs should be comfortable for the writing position, and for sessions of as long as three or four hours. There should be gangway space of at least 5′ everywhere, and open shelves should not be higher overall than 6′. The librarian's desk should allow oversight of the room, and be near the entrance and also the catalogues. The librarian should have ready access to a good selection of subject bibliographies.

Other general requirements are good lighting, natural and artificial, and efficient heating and ventilation.

2. *Lending Department.* In lending libraries, height of shelves, position of entrance and catalogues, minimum size of gangways, heating, lighting and ventilation, are desirably the same as those described for reference libraries. Much is governed by the shape and size of the room, and this, in turn, is governed by the shape of the site. As already indicated, a minimum size for a lending library is 1,200 to 1,600 square feet, which will take a bookstock of 8,000 to 12,000 books arranged on shelves round the walls, and in standard stacks which should not be higher than 5′ 6″. If all windows are at a height of 6′ from the floor, all the wall space can be shelved to that height, and the lowest shelf should be 2′ from the floor. Staff enclosures and counters vary in shape—some are rectangular, some straight, some rounded. They are fitted to take returned books, and to hold the charges of books on loan—bookcards and readers' tickets, one of which is a card and the other a pocket to hold it—which are kept in shallow trays

holding about 100 each. Sometimes these trays are arranged in order of dates in a line; sometimes they are kept on a turntable which can be rotated to bring any tray to the hands of a seated assistant.

The general system of working is for books to carry a label with a distinguishing number, and spaces for stamping the date of issue or of return of the book. These particulars direct the assistant to the charge in the issue trays, which is extracted, thus cancelling the loan, and releasing the reader to obtain whichever new book he requires. Entrance to the library is usually controlled by the assistant behind the counter who, by operating a lever, releases the bolt which locks the entrance wicket. A similar procedure in reverse order is used for issuing books to readers. They surrender the books they wish to borrow and their tickets to the assistant, who extracts the bookcard from each book, stamps the date on the label and, handing the book back to the reader, releases the lock on the exit wicket gate.

An important feature of lending libraries is that there should be enough space between floor stacks to allow easy passage and avoid overcrowding. This means a minimum width of 5' 6", but more space should be allowed wherever possible. The catalogue most in use is the card catalogue, in convenient cabinets and sited to be equally accessible to readers and staff. Many libraries have special display cases and stands for subject exhibitions.

Queues of readers at the entrance counter are inevitable at specially busy periods, but the number of members of the staff on duty should always be enough to prevent undue delay.

Experiments are now being conducted with the

punched card and machines operated by electric power to speed up the processes of issue and return of books. At present, the high cost of the machines makes the system impracticable; but developments may become possible in the future, should costs decrease. Card sorting can be done in this way with incredible speed and complete accuracy.

3. *Children's Libraries.* The children's library is is arranged on similar lines to those of the lending library. The shelves and furniture generally are not as high as those planned for the use of adults; and the arrangement of books on the shelves is better by broad subject grouping rather than strict classified order. It is most desirable for children to have their own accommodation for two main reasons: first, children and adults do not mix happily, as the quick and excitable movements of children are disturbing to many adults; secondly, it is desirable to have a smaller bookstock, and that specially selected, for the use of children. Age of admittance should be elastic, and should depend on ability and desire to use the library rather than age in years. Of particular importance is the children's librarian, who must possess two essential qualities—a good, first-hand knowledge of children's books, particularly those in her own library, and a liking for children and the ability to control them.

4. *School Libraries Department.* Not all libraries have a school libraries department, but it is the custom in some places for the education committee to make a grant to the libraries committee for the purchase of books to supply small libraries to the schools in the town. This is particularly desirable in the case of schools whose

children live half a mile or more from the nearest junior library. One of two systems is followed: either schools have a permanent bookstock, drawn from the pool-stock at the school libraries department, or they draw a loan collection which they return at intervals of six or twelve months, when they borrow another collection. Renovation of bookstock—repairs and rebinding—are arranged by the department, which also keeps statistics of use. Grants of money from education committee to libraries committee rank for Ministry of Education grants.

5. *Commercial and Technical Libraries.* These are part of the reference library work, budded off from the main work of the department to give the best possible service to the trade and industry of the town. They are only to be found in the large towns as, in smaller towns, there is not sufficient of this type of work to justify the creation of a separate department. The stock comprises books, periodicals, trade-catalogues, cuttings from periodicals and other ephemeral publications and, indeed, everything bearing on local industries and trades likely to be of current use. The department must be conveniently situated for the business part of the town, and sometimes is housed separately from the main library building for this purpose. Where there is a Chamber of Commerce for the town, there should be close contact between library and chamber.

6. *Music and Drama Libraries.* The great interest in the two art forms, music and drama, and the special arrangements required for shelving and storage and for the convenience of those making use of the collections, have led to the establishment in some of the larger libraries of separate or joint music and drama libraries,

such as the Henry Watson Music Library at Manchester. The addition to music library stock of gramophone records and facilities for testing them; and the provision of a piano for trying over piano scores, as at Liverpool, call for sound-proof rooms and, in the case of gramophone records, special facilities for storage.

The drama libraries often make a feature of providing 'play sets,' that is, of allowing a sufficient number of copies of separate plays to be borrowed by drama societies who are reading or producing any particular play for each of the 'characters' to have an individual copy.

Movement in this direction in libraries is not yet general, but the influences exerted by the B.B.C. concerts, by the symphony concerts, by the industrial music clubs and other agencies for music; and by the theatre itself and the local drama societies, now so very numerous, make it desirable that the public needs should be met in the libraries; though whether through establishing separate departments or by expanding the general stock in these special subjects is a matter for local decision.

7. *Visual Aids Department.* The visual aids department is a new departure in public library practice, and is only to be found in large town and county libraries. The stock of the department consists of pictures, prints and illustrative material generally; and also cinema films, film strips and lantern slides. It is a service used largely by schoolteachers, and also by all societies conducting lecture courses. The material is in the main used to illustrate lectures and talks.

8. *Cataloguing Department.* The cataloguing department is also a feature of large libraries. Where there is

bookstock passing into a library or system of libraries which is enough to require the full-time work of two or more persons, it is desirable to place this work in the charge of a qualified librarian, with such assistance as is necessary. A large library with a central and several branch libraries, and most county libraries, can only achieve uniform treatment of books, so desirable in practice, by centralising the work.

9. *Branch Libraries Department.* A separate branch libraries department is necessary only when the system has six or more branch libraries. Its work, supervised and organised by the superintendent of branch libraries, is to select and arrange interchange of branch libraries stock, and to co-ordinate the branch libraries' work with each other and with the central library. Purchase of stock, after selection, will be carried out in the accessions department, and its cataloguing and classification in the cataloguing department. It has been a general custom for branches with a stock of 5,000 or more books to have each an individual stock, increased by weekly additions, and pruned at regular intervals. County libraries have made a notable contribution to this procedure. County branches have a basic stock, but also make regular changes of popular stock to their sub-branches, as to their smaller units, the village centres. This is desirable for all branch libraries, and regular interchanges of popular stock are becoming general in branch library method. The system is to have a central pool-stock, as with school libraries, and for branches to exchange part of their stocks by drawing on the pool at half-yearly intervals. It is important that branch libraries should not work in watertight compartments, but should interweave their

work with that of the other units of the service to which they belong, and the officer responsible for this correlation is the superintendent of branch libraries.

10. *Further Education Department.* This department exists to arrange book loans to classes and study groups, whether they are part of the organised education service of the area or not. It may be a sub-department of the central lending library, but it is desirable that it should have its own bookstock. Any adult or evening class, whether of the local education authority, Workers' Educational Association, or other teaching body, should be able to borrow a collection of books for the use of class members, issued to it for the period of the class or for an academic session. Some local education authorities make a grant for the purchase of books for this purpose to the local libraries committee. A separate bookstock is most desirable, as the books required are often those in steady demand in lending libraries, and it would be unfair to the general body of readers to reserve them for special groups over a long period, which is the ordinary requirement in this class of work. Grants from local education authorities to library committees for this purpose rank for Ministry of Education grant.

11. *Administration Department.* Administrative work must be carried out in all libraries. In the small libraries it will be done mainly by the librarian himself. It is concerned with day to day business, organisation of duties, the employment of staff, holiday arrangements, correspondence, organization of lectures and exhibitions, preparation of business for committee meetings, and so on. It is, in short, the business office or offices of the library and, in the larger library systems, the quantity of

detailed work required needs a separate department and staff to deal with it. Acquisition of bookstock and its registration may either be dealt with by this department or by a separate Accessions Department.

12. *Photographic Department.* This will only be found in large libraries. The equipment required is a photostat, or other machine for copying documents, and the necessary apparatus to make microfilm. Most libraries possess material which they are not prepared to lend, and in large libraries, with considerable manuscript, rare book and pamphlet stock, calls to lend this material to other towns are frequent. It is now possible to make photographic copies either in facsimile or, particularly for items with more than twelve folios, in miniature (microfilm). The latter requires a special apparatus to enable readers to read it, which should now become an ordinary item of reference library equipment.

Work of this kind requires expert treatment, qualified staff, and specially fitted accommodation, but it is work which is increasing in output and importance, and smaller libraries can often make use of apparatus in other corporation departments when it would obviously be uneconomic to establish their own department for this purpose.

13. *Stores Department.* This is another of the departments only to be found in the larger systems. Stores bulk considerably when there are a dozen or more separate buildings, and they range from lead pencils to spare parts for vacuum cleaners. All purchases should be accounted for, and all giving out of stores carefully recorded. The best system is to have a card for each

item ruled to take particulars of quantity, supplier, price and issue. Arrangements should be made to hold a reserve stock of all items, to prevent any possibility of running out of stock.

14. *Publicity Department.* This is a development of the future, as it is doubtful if any British library has, as yet, established such a department. Our publicity methods are much behind the times. Only a small proportion of the population of any town or county knows the capabilities of the library service, and publicity work at present, carried out in what time can be spared from essential duties, is haphazard and unsatisfactory. There is a possibility of national publicity being initiated by the Library Association through the appointment of a public relations officer, and if this desirable development takes place, it will be certain of good results; but local publicity is equally important and, at least in the larger cities, may lead to special treatment, which can have its due effect on all the smaller towns in the surrounding area. Many hold that the best of all publicity is efficient service.

15. *Bindery.* Few libraries have a full binding department able to carry out all the binding work of the library, but, though it may cost a little more than sending work out to contractors, it has many advantages. The minimum staff is two men, one woman and two girl sewers, for a department to be effective, and binding equipment is at present in very short supply. Libraries which have not sufficient work to justify the necessary staff are well advised to make use of the special library binding contractors.

CHAPTER VII

BOOKSTOCK: 1—SELECTION, ACCESSIONING AND PROCESSING

(a) *Book Selection.* The selection of bookstock for libraries calls for both knowledge and experience. In small libraries it is usually carried out by the chief librarian; in large libraries by the senior staff in charge of departments, supervised and co-ordinated by the chief librarian. Requirements include bibliographies and catalogues, and it is most desirable to consult experts in special subjects for detailed guidance. Here it is proposed to deal only with the routine processes of book selection; theory and practice must be pursued in the special textbooks which treat of the subject, e.g. L. R. McColvin's *Library Stock,* J. H. Wellard's *Book Selection* and Helen Haines's *Living with Books.* Young librarians should make a practice of reading book reviews in the *Times Literary Supplement* and those weekly periodicals which make a feature of keeping their readers in touch with recent publications. For current literature the essential reference books are *The [American] Cumulative Book Index,* published by The Wilson Book Co.; the *English Catalogue of Books* (annual), published by The Publishers' Circular, Whitaker's *Cumulative Book List,* and the weekly publications, the *Publishers' Circular,* and the *Bookseller.*

The routine of book selection divides into two branches —that concerned with selection of stock for new libraries, mainly branch libraries, and that concerned

BOOK SELECTION, ACCESSIONING, PROCESSING

with the replenishment and revision of the stock of existing libraries.

For the first of these, selection for new libraries—remembering the general book shortage which is a feature of the present time—the librarian begins by considering the size of the library and the relation of this to the potential number of readers. It was discovered in the early days of county library organisation that small libraries require a higher proportion of fiction and the lighter forms of reading than the larger libraries, and the relative proportions of light and serious books—usually fiction and non-fiction—range from 80 per cent light and 20 per cent serious in the smallest libraries to the reverse of this in large libraries. This problem, and that of subjects to be represented in the stock, and by which books, call for careful study; but the attempt made in the past to formulate proportions of books in the main classes of literature—a certain percentage to philosophy, to religion, to sociology, and so on—is not in practice successful, nor is it any longer seriously advocated. One factor is constant, however, namely, that the smaller the library, the greater the need to obtain a high standard of readability in the books provided. What constitutes 'readability' is the subject of much argument; but its practical significance is demonstrated by the use or disuse of the books in any library. In an established library, much can be deduced from analysing periodically the use made of what has been provided, and keeping careful records of requests for named books, and books on named subjects; but in a new library to serve an area hitherto unserved, selection in the first instance must be experimental, the only bounds being the knowledge of the librarian and the state of the book market. Help in selecting older books may be obtained from many sources, e.g. Munford's *Basic Stock*, and the Library Association's *Books for Youth*.

Book selection for replenishment and revision of stock should include provision of facilities for an adequate system of changing stock which, in the smallest of libraries, may involve complete exchanges three or four times a year, and in the larger ones a partial exchange at regular intervals. No useful purpose is served by taking away a book from a library while it is in demand; and, equally true, it is undesirable to leave a book in a library for longer than a year if it is not receiving any use. To maintain exchanges of this kind requires a pool stock—for centres and branches in county libraries, for branches and sub-branches in town libraries; and the regular and sufficient adding to such pool stock should be systematic and of adequate proportions.

The town with one library only, the central library of a town with central and branches, and the county library headquarters, feeding branches and centres, and with its students' section, share the same principles of routine book selection. All will select for purchase books of special local significance, and the outstanding publications in popular reading—fiction, travel, biography, politics and the arts and sciences. In the small libraries, duplication of titles will be unusual; in the larger libraries, the estimate of the number of copies which should be purchased of books likely to be in great demand calls for careful consideration. Actual numbers vary from two or three to as many as one hundred. What needs to be decided is the number of copies necessary to satisfy reasonable demands which will, all of them, be used sufficiently to warrant their purchase. If the number bought of copies of any title is too great, this will mean wastage of the book fund; if too few, inadequacy of service. The larger libraries select books for purchase on a wider basis than the smaller, as their book stock can absorb several books covering the same ground in different ways, whereas the smaller library may only have use for one, and must decide with care which of the several that may be available is likely to be most suitable. Calls made on the bookstock of the larger libraries are likely to cover a wider field of learning than those made on smaller libraries, and this point also requires careful attention. One other essential requirement in selecting new books is a detailed knowledge of the library stock and of the main reading trends of the public making use of it. The actual selection is made from publishers' lists, trade papers, and periodicals containing reviews of new books, and, as stated, it is work usually shared by the senior members of the staff.

These are the principles which guide and direct book selection in libraries. The practice is a constant one, comprising the study of new publications and selection from them, the consideration of suggestions made by readers, and revision of existing stock, withdrawal of the out-of-date, and replenishment and augmentation by the addition of new editions and of books, possibly quite old publications, not previously in the library, for which there appears to be a need.

When books have been selected for purchase, it is usual to write particulars of them on stock cards, which are often ruled to give spaces for author's name, title, date of publication, publisher, edition, number of volumes, date of selection and of purchase, whether to be bought new or secondhand and from whom, the published price and the actual price paid by the library. Sometimes spaces are also included to show date of rebinding and of withdrawal.

In some libraries the chief officer has power of book purchase, either unlimited or limited. In others, proposed purchases must be approved by the library committee, a possible procedure for small libraries, but impossible for large systems, and undesirable for all. Discretion of purchase should always be in the hands of the chief librarian, who knows better than any one what is required and will, without prompting, refer doubtful points to his committee for decision, particularly when scarce and costly items are in question.

Libraries usually have regular suppliers to whom book orders are dispatched on some pre-arranged plan. It is a great convenience if the suppliers are local tradesmen, but some librarians prefer to deal with large non-local bookstores which make a speciality of supplying public libraries. Approved libraries in membership with the Library Association are entitled to a book licence which allows booksellers named in the licence to give a discount on books bought (with certain infrequent exceptions) of 10% off the published prices.

(b) *Accessioning of bookstock.* The old method of keeping records of accessions of books, still in use in some of the older libraries, was to have ledgers ruled into columns to give the following or similar particulars—running number, date of invoice, author, title, number of volumes, publisher, price, donor or vendor. To these other columns were sometimes added, to show particulars of subject, of edition, and of binding and date of withdrawal or replacement. The register of accessions in this form was a complete stock history of the library, and there is much to be said for it. There is also a good deal against it—it requires to be handwritten, and handwriting varies in legibility and tidiness, and it takes up much time in its compilation. A simplified form on the loose-leaf ledger principle, with similar columns, but to be used with a typewriter, is quicker, neater and easier to work with. Some booksellers are prepared to supply their invoices in the form of loose leaves perforated for filing in a ledger, and to send them in duplicate, so that one can be forwarded for payment to the treasurer and the other retained by the library as its accessions register, and some libraries make considerable use of this service. Others treat the stock cards prepared as part of the routine of book selection as their accessions register, by adding a running number to them when the books are received, and filing them in numerical order. The running number, or accession number, is added to the book to which it applies, usually on the back of the title-page. It is desirable to write it on another page also, in case the title-page may be removed or lost.

It is a matter for local decision which form of register of accessions shall be used; but it is suggested that an initial saving of staff time may be purchased too dearly. Accuracy of entries is imperative, and it is fatally easy to make mistakes in copying book details, as those who have experience in checking cataloguing attempts by beginners know only too well. The work of accessioning books is an important part of library routine. It should be in the hands of an experienced and trained person, and the form recommended is the loose-leaf ledger compiled in the library.

(c) *Book-processing*. Processing is the term applied to the carrying out of the details of preparing books for shelving with the general stock, and issuing them to readers. Full processing includes collating, stamping, cutting the paper folds or 'bolts' when the edges have not been trimmed off by a cutting machine called a guillotine, pasting in rules and date labels or bookplates, preparing book issue cards and pasting in the envelopes or pockets to contain them, and marking class or division numbers or letters on the book-backs (or spines).

In recent library practice 'processing' has been very closely scrutinised by librarians in order to eliminate any unnecessary work, as a feeling had grown that library method in connection with bookstock was too elaborate, and took up too much staff time which could be used to better purpose in more important duties.

To collate a book is to check its make-up to see that it is in perfect condition, that it contains its full number of pages in their right order, with none omitted or duplicated; that the illustrations are all in their correct places as detailed in the list printed as part of the preliminaries in the book; that the book is properly cased or bound and not cased back to front, and that all the parts listed in the table of contents are as stated.

Library ownership is signified by stamping a name-stamp of the library in the book in certain prescribed places, e.g. on the back of the title-page, on the back of plates, on the top edges of the book, or wherever it has been decided locally that the stamp is to appear. Usually a round rubber stamp is used with black, green or red ink. Sometimes an embossing stamp is used which makes a relief impression without ink.

Edge-cutting or opening is not often required, as most

books are published with their edges trimmed and the folds or bolts removed. In the few cases where this is not so, an ordinary bone paper knife should be used, and it is necessary to point out to all beginners that the fold which ends at the spine of the book must be cut to its full length, otherwise the uncut portion will tear in a most unsightly way when the book is opened for reading.

Pasting in of book-plates and of rules and date-labels is a simple matter, but those who do it should be careful to make a neat job by seeing that the edges of pasted labels are parallel to the book-edges, and that the minimum only of paste is used, and any surplus wiped off before the book is closed.

Book issue cards are usually made to fit into a paste-on envelope on the inside of the front board of the book. The cards are of various sizes; but $4'' \times 2''$ is a useful size. They have written on them book number, author and title, and some indication of the subject of the book, either its classification number or an abbreviation of this.

Lettering of class or other numbers on the spines of books is best done in gold leaf by a binder's finisher. It is not necessary with novels, as these are usually shelved in alphabetical order of authors' names, which should always be printed on the book spines. This cover title must contain sufficient information to enable the books to be shelved expeditiously, and the shelf arrangement to be checked with equal speed and accuracy. It is a convenience to stamp class marks in all cases at an even distance from the heel of the spine—say $1\frac{1}{2}$ or 2 inches —and the superiority of gold stamping by a trained binder's finisher over all other methods is unquestionable. Though it is not impossible for library assistants to learn to do this work, the time absorbed and the frequently imperfect results obtained by amateurs make it uneconomical and undesirable that it should be attempted by other than craftsmen. Other methods of book-numbering are used in some libraries, mainly hand lettering with an electrically heated pen printing the marks through a metal foil on to the book spines. This method can be very effective when carried out by a person who is able to write letters and figures clearly, uniformly and of even size; it can also be untidy and unsightly when badly done. The use of ordinary inks for book lettering is undesirable, as they cannot be applied evenly and do not last any length of time.

Speed and accuracy of book accessioning and processing are essential in good library method, as they control the flow of additions to the stock. This flow should be regular in quantity, and not a matter of fits and starts. The cataloguing department is fed from the processing department, just as the processing department is fed from the accessions department; and these, in turn, determine the flow of new acquisitions to the shelves of the library and so to the hands and homes of readers. It is because of the need to speed the passing of books from bookshop to library shelves that changes from the older and more leisurely methods of book processing have been adopted in many libraries. Novels are now seldom collated: in fact some libraries omit collation of books altogether, considering that deficiencies in make-up are so few that checking is unnecessary. Name-stamping is also omitted sometimes; and book-cards may have no other particular than the number necessary for issue charges. Certainly this saves staff time in process work; but when books are lost, or kept over time by readers, and it becomes necessary to write letters about them, or to identify them as library property, the initial saving of time through cutting out process details may be found to be a doubtful economy or, indeed, no economy at all.

CHAPTER VIII

BOOKSTOCK: 2—CLASSIFICATION

THE classification of books in libraries is carried out for one main purpose, namely to enable readers and staff to find books on the shelves as required. In its practice it accomplishes much besides this main function: it brings all the books in the library on each subject together, and surrounds them with other books on related subjects; it introduces the reader who goes to the shelves for one particular book to others on the same subject; it facilitates search for particularised information; and it expedites the periodical surveys of library bookstock which are necessary to keep it abreast of the times. It also has a personal virtue for those who are in contact with it in their daily life, as it assists the processes of mental observation and reasoning.

Even the smallest library needs to have some settled plan of shelf arrangement; indeed, it is this process of arrangement which distinguishes a library from a mere collection of miscellaneous volumes. The contrast can be well appreciated if the contents of the average secondhand bookshop are compared with the contents of a well organised library.

It is a useful introduction to the subject of book classification in libraries to consider briefly some of the older methods of shelf arrangement. One of the earliest was to number each tier of book shelves, and each of the shelves in each of the tiers—the tiers might be A, B, C and so on, and the shelves 1, 2, 3 and so on, counting from the top shelf downwards. As the books were placed on the shelves, they also were numbered 1, 2, 3, etc., counting from left to right. A book might thus bear the symbol C, 4, 16, which would signify that it was to be found in the third tier, on the fourth shelf, and was the sixteenth book on that shelf. With this system there could be no changing round of books on the shelves, as this would mean complete alteration of all book symbols; it was, in fact, a system of rigid location; and there was no attempt at bringing books on the same subject together, as they were simply given the first empty place on the shelves in the order of their acquisition.

Such rigidity of shelf arrangement as this caused great waste of time in assembling together as required a selection of books on any particular subject, and it was followed by a primitive system of subject order. Each of the main classes into which knowledge may be divided was given a letter of the alphabet—A, B, C, etc.—as a symbol for that class, and the books in it were given a running number as they were acquired for the library, e.g. the book with the symbol A 405 would be the four hundred and fifth book acquired by the library in subject A. This arrangement was a great improvement on the earlier rigid shelf arrangement, as books could be moved from one shelf to another so long as the numerical arrangement inside the subject classes was maintained.

Arrangement in main classes in order of accessions to the library continued in library practice for many years, and was still common between 1910 and 1920. But during the last quarter of the nineteenth century much inquiry and experiment on the subject of book classification had taken place, mainly in America, where the two chief experimenters and exponents were Melvil Dewey and Charles A. Cutter. Both invented a scheme of subject classification for books, but that of Dewey was much preferred to his rival's and, from its first appearance in 1876, it has continued to give general satisfaction, and in process of time has grown from a work of pamphlet size of no more than sixteen pages to its present great bulk of 1,927 pages. Other schemes that have found some favour are the Subject Classification of the English librarian James Duff Brown, and the classification of the American Library of Congress.

All schemes of book classification must be based on some system of the classification or ordering of knowledge as reasoned and described by philosophers. An important part of the work of philosophers is that devoted to the science of logic, and to study the subject of book classification intelligently it is necessary to spend some time initially in learning the elements of logic, or the science of reasoning, as first conceived by the Greek philosopher Aristotle. To pursue this course, two works have been used by librarians for many years, both of them by Professor William Stanley Jevons (1835–82), who was for some time professor of logic and political economy at Owen's College, Manchester, and later professor of political economy at University College, London. The two works are: his small book, *Elementary Lessons in Logic*, first published in 1870, which should be read throughout; and his *Principles of Science*, a major work first published in 1873, of which it is necessary to read only Chapter XXX, which deals with classification. In this latter work appears a definition of classification which should be memorised. It was composed by Huxley, the famous zoologist, and appeared in his *Lectures on the Elements of Comparative Anatomy*, from which it is quoted by Jevons. The definition is as follows: "By the classification of any series of objects, is meant the actual or ideal arrangement together of those which are like, and the separation of those which are unlike; the purpose of this arrangement being to facilitate the operations of the mind in clearly conceiving and retaining in the memory the characters of the objects in question."

Although, as already indicated, schemes for the classification of books must be based on the classification of knowledge, they need not, and indeed do not follow plans which would be accepted by logicians. The prime needs of successful schemes of book classification are well appreciated by those who work in libraries; they are, first, that they must provide placings for all books in all subjects; secondly, that the headings allotted to subjects must not overlap, and each heading must exclude all others, or (as expressed by Berwick Sayers, whose books on classification must be studied by all librarians) they must be mutually exclusive; thirdly, that they must make provision for books in which the form of writing is more important than the subject matter, e.g. novels, poetry and drama; fourthly, that they must make provision for the treatment of books which deal with many subjects; fifthly, that they must make provision for the unlimited interpolation of new headings at any point; sixthly, that they must be provided with a system of symbols, one for each heading, which are as flexible as the headings themselves and can be added to wherever and whenever necessary (this is known as the notation of the scheme); and seventhly, that they must be provided with an index in alphabetical order of all headings, including all synonyms for the names used in the tables of headings.

With the foregoing details as an introduction, it is the duty of Library Association examination candidates to study the Decimal classification by Dewey, first to gain an understanding of the scheme itself, and then to see how far it answers the requirements of librarians; though this need not be taken too seriously, as the widespread use of this scheme in libraries all over the world is a sufficient indication that, at least in large measure, it does satisfy the needs of librarians. The approach to the study of Dewey's scheme should be the careful reading and re-reading of the Introduction to the work itself. In this will be found a thorough and very clear description of the principles on which the scheme is framed, the order pursued, the method of compiling the notation and index, and many other details; and as the study of these details proceeds, the main order of the classes and of the numbers given to symbolise them become memorised, a process of much more lasting virtue than the attempt sometimes made to memorise without thought, as a child learns a recitation. However much memorising of numbers for subjects may be accomplished, this is of little value if it is not informed by an understanding of the processes of compilation. It is, in short, necessary to understand the scheme, not to memorise it or any part of it; such memorising as there may be of symbols and subjects should be incidental and not deliberate.

The method of dealing with books too general in content to allow them to be classified by subject is an important feature of book classification which can be dealt with appropriately either at the beginning or at the end of the scheme. Dewey, as will be seen, deals with it initially, and includes with the obvious works of this type, such as encyclopædias, books on the science of librarianship, which pervades all knowledge. Also included in this category of books about books are bibliographies and catalogues—those important tools of librarians and research workers—and general indexes, including those dealing with periodical literature, such as the Library Association's *Subject Index to Periodicals*.

The next point of importance to call for notice is the method of dealing with books written or compiled in a particular form which may be more important to readers than is the subject matter. The Decimal classification meets this by having separate 'form' classes and divisions. The 'forms' which are allotted main classes in the scheme are poetry, drama, essays, fiction, and other less important ones. The form divisions which pervade the scheme include dictionaries, encyclopædias, compendiums and essays. It will be found that an encyclopædia which deals with all subject matter goes in the generalia class; but an encyclopædia or dictionary of chemistry is classed with the books on that subject. Similarly, a book of general essays on a variety of miscellaneous topics is placed in the general class if the essays are informative; if they are intended to be read for æsthetic enjoyment, they are classified in the form class for essays in the language in which they are printed; but a book of essays on the subject of chemistry is classified with other books on chemistry. The notation of the scheme includes symbols which allow these form distinctions to be indicated in the classification numbers allotted to the books to which they apply. How these things are done is fully explained in the introduction to the work.

Another point of importance is the method provided to indicate location. The main class which deals with geography, topography and history provides placings for all these topics for all the countries in the world. But it is also necessary to provide a method of taking locality into account when considering special subjects, e.g. the birds of Britain, or the flowers of South America. The method provided is that the geographical numbers for these countries, and all others, or abbreviations of them, may be added in a certain prescribed way to the specific subject numbers. In the case of books on birds of Britain, the number to be allotted is the subject number for birds in the division zoology, to which is added the geographical number for Britain taken from the main class dealing with history and geography.

Yet another important feature of a good book classification scheme is a satisfactory method of dealing with books that treat of more than one subject, though these are within a prescribed field of knowledge. Examples are books dealing with algebra, geometry and trigonometry, or beetles, butterflies and wasps. The method to be followed is to place them at a point in the scheme which is as specific as possible, but wide enough to contain all that the book includes, i.e. in the first example, under the general heading 'mathematics,' and in the second under the heading 'insects.' Books are sometimes written on subjects which cannot be covered by one general heading, as for example, architecture and building, when the book must be classed under the subject which receives fuller treatment than the other, and the necessary linking up must be left to the catalogue. Related to this point is the method to be adopted with books on specific subjects, but written from a standpoint which may be almost as important as the subject matter: examples of this are books on the psychology of education, or the law of workmen's compensation. Here there is a choice of placings to be made, but the general library will classify the books where they will be required—the psychology of education with the books on education, and the law of workmen's compensation with the books on other matters concerned with labour.

As no one who uses a book classification scheme of the magnitude of that of Dewey could ever know intimately more than a part of it, the index is essential to its use. There are two kinds of index: first, the specific index, which gives one entry only to each topic; secondly, the relative index, as provided with the Decimal classification, which adds to all subjects indexed a series of standpoints from which the subject may be considered. In the first of these, the subject 'flowers' would have one entry only; in the second, standpoints would be indicated, e.g. botany, use of flowers in heraldry, or in symbolism, or as table decoration, etc. This feature of the relative type of index is most useful to classifiers, and is a great saver of time. It is possible to allot subject marks to books by using the alphabetical subject index alone; but this is very unwise. The correct method is to refer to the index when required, and then to turn to the subject number given by the index in the main tables of the scheme to see just exactly what is given there. It may be found that the index number is the appropriate one; on the other hand, it may be found that, for the particular book concerned, a more general or a more specific number is desirable. These are matters of great importance in the practice of classifying books for a library.

Many libraries using the Decimal classification adopt certain variations. Some do not use the scheme fully, but use a simplified version which is obtainable. Others, while using most of the scheme as it appears, adopt variations in classing biography, using a simplified method of arranging all biographies in one alphabetical sequence of names of persons written about, instead of the Dewey method of arranging them according to the positions they held or the work they did. Most libraries keep fiction apart from the classification scheme altogether.

The study of classification, either in itself or in its relation to books, can be a fascinating one; and it is a subject to which all librarians must give much attention. Moreover, a good knowledge of one scheme, such as that of Dewey, is the best possible way of understanding other schemes.

CHAPTER IX

BOOKSTOCK: 3—CATALOGUING

A LIBRARY without a catalogue is like a country without a map: the one supplies the information as to which books are included in the library stock, and where they may be found; the other plots the positions of towns and other geographical features, and the roads which lead to them. A traveller in either fares badly without such aid, but he is quick to realise that there are good and bad maps, and equally that there are good and bad catalogues.

In libraries in which readers are not admitted to the bookshelves, the catalogue is the only guide. In open-access libraries, the system common in all public lending libraries, guidance to the bookshelves by shelf labels is usually provided, and many readers find that this shelf guidance meets their needs, and they make little or no use of the catalogue. Because of this it is sometimes argued that an open-access library does not need a catalogue, and that to provide one is an unnecessary expenditure of money and of staff time; but it must be pointed out that the open shelf part of most libraries contains at any given time only a portion of the bookstock—many books are out on loan; others may be shelved in a reserve department because of the limited shelf capacity of the open-access department; some may be temporarily removed for repair or rebinding. Only from the catalogue can the full resources in any subject be ascertained.

An opinion is held by many librarians that, though

there is adequate reason for having a catalogue of the non-fiction bookstock, there is not the same need for a catalogue of the fiction holdings. Much fiction, they point out, has a comparatively brief life in the library, and is not replaced when worn out; and it is not a matter of much importance which, of many novels, may be borrowed. The need, or otherwise, of a catalogue of fiction is a matter for local decision.

In reference libraries the catalogue is essential, as the proportion of calls for specific books is high and, particularly in the larger libraries, the number of books on open shelves is small compared with the number not on open shelves. It is also necessary in reference libraries to catalogue all books in considerable detail, as only by doing so can readers be given proper assistance.

A main consideration in the work of cataloguing books is that of consistency, for without this there must follow constant vexation and feelings of frustration. To enter English names with the prefix 'de' sometimes under the prefix and sometimes under what follows it, or to be guilty of other inconsistencies, would completely destroy faith in the efficacy of the catalogue; and inconsistency through many possible variations in treatment is constantly found in catalogues compiled by amateurs and without system.

It was the need for systematic treatment which inspired the compilation of codes of cataloguing rules, several of which are now in use. The British Museum and the Bodleian Library have their own codes; a code was drawn up by the American librarian Charles A. Cutter for use in making dictionary catalogues; and another was compiled by a joint committee of English and American librarians, which is called *Cataloguing Rules,*

Author and Title Entries, and is usually referred to as the Anglo-American code. It is this latter—the Anglo-American code—which is in greatest use in English libraries, and it is on this that the examinations of the Library Association are framed.

There are several types of catalogue in use, including the author catalogue, the dictionary catalogue, the classified catalogue and the alphabetical-subject catalogue. All have their advantages and disadvantages. The author catalogue gives all necessary particulars so long as the name of the author of the required book is known, but does not help those who wish to ascertain the library holdings on any particular subject. The dictionary catalogue arranges entries of books under names of authors and again under specific subject headings in one alphabetical sequence, and is the form of catalogue preferred in the United States. Its defect is that books on any wide field of knowledge are separated in entry according to the letters of the alphabet—books on botany, for example, are to be found under the headings flowers, shrubs, trees, ferns, and so on, as well as under the heading botany, and though they are linked by cross-references, much work is involved in assembling details of library holdings on any required subject. The alphabetical-classed catalogue attempts to overcome the subject difficulty of the dictionary catalogue by arranging entries alphabetically under main subject headings with sub-divisions, and with references from specific subject names to the more general headings. For example, all the books on botany appear under this main heading, divided into parts bearing sub-headings (flowers, shrubs, etc.); and under the word 'flowers' at letter F in the alphabet, the searcher is directed for books on this subject to the heading botany, sub-heading flowers. The main fault of this form of catalogue is that the choice of headings is arbitrary, and related subjects are distributed through the whole alphabet. The classified catalogue, to be satisfactory, requires to be in three separate parts—classified section, author index and subject index—as compared with the dictionary catalogue's single and comprehensive sequence, and it is therefore a form which has to be learned, whereas the dictionary form is known by all, and requires no instruction in its use. The classified catalogue, in spite of this defect as compared with the dictionary catalogue, is the type preferred in England, and it is used in most public libraries.

Library catalogues are of several kinds, i.e. printed, manuscript, typescript; book, card and sheaf. The most easily used kind is the printed catalogue, but it is expensive to produce and is out of date before it can be published.[1] The manuscript catalogue in books or on sheets kept together in covers is suitable only for the smallest libraries, as interpolation of entries is progressively more and more difficult as sheets become filled with entries, and any exact order of arrangement cannot be maintained. The card catalogue, either typed or manuscript, is the most popular form, and has much in common with the sheaf catalogue. In compiling card catalogues, cards of a standard size, usually 5" × 3", are used, and no card is used to describe more than a single book, which permits complete flexibility of arrangement, and allows for interpolation at any point and at any time. In compiling sheaf catalogues, paper sheets of

---

[1] Though this is true of the ordinary town or county library, printed catalogues of comprehensive and special libraries (e.g. The British Museum Catalogue, and that of the London School of Economics) are invaluable tools of the librarian.

a convenient size are used, usually a little larger than that of the standard card size, and the sheets, when completed, are arranged on the loose-leaf system in cloth folders.

The treatment of books in the process of cataloguing cannot be left to chance. The results of this—or some of them—have already been indicated and, as also indicated, codes of cataloguing rules have been compiled and are in regular use. It is not of particular practical importance which of the available codes is chosen; but in British public libraries the code usually preferred is the one sponsored by the Library Association—the Anglo-American. To its use must be added system and method of work, as the orderliness and neatness which this engenders are important features in library practice. It is often suggested by inexperienced persons that the practice of cataloguing can be carried out by any intelligent person without instruction or guidance, and they point to a supposed similarity between library cataloguing and making an inventory of the furniture of a house, or any other form of listing or docketing.

Even a very limited experience either in compiling or using a well-compiled library catalogue is sufficient to dispel any such view, particularly when the different forms of authorship of books are studied. The author of a book may be a single person, or two or more persons writing in collaboration; or may be something quite different. The author is the originator, and may be personal or impersonal. A society, which is the originator of its proceedings or transactions is, in this sense, the author of them; and an institution is the author of the publications issued in its name; and, similarly, a Corporation, or municipal borough, or government department. The statutes of a country originate from its legislative body—again authorship; the trade catalogue of a firm of manufacturers originates from the firm. These and many other problems of authorship are the daily fare of the library cataloguer, and each and all of them must receive similarity of treatment with its type, or the result will be chaos.

Other problems arise in connection with persons who have more than one name, for example, a nobleman with a title and also a family name; with dignitaries of Church or State, who may have both personal names and official titles, and be known equally well by either; with persons who write books under an assumed name, or several assumed names, and sometimes under their own names as well; with persons who, for one reason or another, change their names, such as married women, who may be found to write their early works under their maiden names and their later ones under their married names; with persons who change their names by deed poll; with persons who are raised to the peerage. All these and many other matters relating to the authorship of books arise in the day-to-day work of the cataloguer, and they can only be dealt with satisfactorily by adhering to defined and precise rules. Cataloguing, in short, is a very exact science which calls for complete consistency if it is to serve its full and proper purpose.

Some confusion is often experienced by beginners when they first come to use the Anglo-American code which, as already mentioned, bears the title, *Cataloguing Rules, Author and Title Entries*. They know that the catalogue of their library is classified, and wonder how rules for author or title entries can be used to serve the needs of those compiling classified catalogues. As will soon be found in practice, the cataloguing of any book is a process in itself, and the finished product of the cataloguer can be used to serve varying needs: the important point being that the cataloguing process, as carried out, provides adequate descriptions of the books concerned, which may be filed for use in any one of several ways. The stressing of authorship in cataloguing is because, though many other things about any particular book may vary, the author is an unchangeable factor. Things that may vary are date of publication, size, presence or absence of illustrations, title, text as first written, or text with notes by the author or some other person, publication in original language of the book or in translation into another language. All these things may vary in different copies of the same book, but the authorship does not vary, and therefore the author is the keypoint or cornerstone of all book catalogue entries. Once entries for books have been made, their arrangement for use may follow whatever order is decided upon. They may be arranged in alphabetical order of names of authors, or in order of the classification symbols added to the entries; or they may be arranged by place-names of publication, or date of publication, or indeed in whatever order may be required. The important point is that the cataloguing itself is not the deciding feature of the arrangement of the entries.

Catalogues are called upon to answer questions relating to the contents of the libraries to which they apply, as already described (see p. 13). It is a usual practice to systematise the order of making entries when cataloguing books, as it is considered that to follow a definite plan makes for speed and accuracy, and also assists users of the catalogue, who quickly become acquainted with the method used, and when they have done so, are able to form a mental picture of each book of which they read the particulars. The approved method of catalogue entry is to divide it into five parts—author, title, imprint, collation, and annotation or note. These five parts are treated as paragraphs are treated in writing, when card catalogues are being compiled, and sometimes also in printed catalogues, though in the latter, to save printing space and therefore cost, some of the details may be made to run on without beginning a new line. All beginners need to be warned against the fatal ease with which mistakes in copying from title-pages may be made, e.g. Worley for Wortley, Philips for Phillips, and so on. If mistakes are not detected and corrected at the time they are made, they may cause much trouble later on.

Though printed catalogues are now unusual, the printing of select lists and bulletins of recent additions to libraries is a common practice. These vary in size from four-page leaflets to pamphlets of as many as one hundred pages. In some, correct cataloguing method is followed, but in others, particularly the four-page leaflet type, this is often not the case. Printed leaflets and pamphlets serve a dual purpose—first, they advertise some special feature of the library or of its bookstock; and secondly, they draw attention to the library itself. When well done, this form of book-list publicity seems well worth while; but if badly done, it is likely to do more harm than good. Young students of librarianship should make it their business to learn something about printing and type-faces, a subject they will study in greater detail later on. Used as a method of catalogue production there is nothing as good as printing, whether the catalogue is on cards or in book form. There are so many printing type-faces available that, whatever variety of size, design or spacing is required may be obtained.

At present, for British libraries, there is no system of central cataloguing as there is in America, where the Library of Congress produces printed catalogue cards for all books added to its stock, and conducts a worldwide service of supplying copies of these cards at very low cost. A book that has been properly catalogued once does not need to be done a second time; but, lacking the co-operation which comes from a centralised system of cataloguing, the same book in British libraries is catalogued not once or twice, but often hundreds of times. If a central bureau could be established which would supply printed catalogue cards for books as published, the great labour of library cataloguing as practised at the present time would be very considerably reduced, but attempts to establish such a bureau in this country to carry out work as done in America by the Library of Congress have so far proved unavailing. Central cataloguing, it should be added, can only be successful if the cards relating to books are made available within a reasonable time after the date of publication of the books to which they apply, and in America there appears to be a time-lag in this matter. But the time that would be saved if a satisfactory service of this kind could be established is likely to be so considerable that not only does the question call for attention, but everything should be done to provide a satisfactory answer.

The term central cataloguing is sometimes used for the centralised cataloguing of a single library system with a central and branch libraries. This is usually in charge of a trained librarian, with trained librarians as assistants, and sometimes with one or more typists. All the lending library cataloguing for central and branches is done here, which ensures two things—first, that book classification and cataloguing are standardised; secondly, that one treatment serves for the same book in however many libraries it may be placed. A union catalogue of all books in the library system is kept at the central library, each card being marked with symbols to indicate the departments or branches which have a copy of the book catalogued.

Where typists are employed, the cataloguing is done by a trained librarian on a master slip, which is passed to the typist to make the required number of copies on cards for the different card catalogues.

Briefly, this does for a library system what central cataloguing in the wider sense would do for the country as a whole.

All who deal with printing should be familiar with the conventional marks used by printers to distinguish the different sizes and kinds of type—roman, italic, etc.—and the correction of proofs of matter as set up in type. Details of this, and of the marks to be used in making corrections, should be memorised, and are to be found in any book dealing with the elements of the craft of printing.

CHAPTER X

BOOKSTOCK: 4—CARE OF STOCK, REVISION, STOCKTAKING

THE importance of being able to find any book in the stock of a library, and the methods adopted to ensure that this can be done with reasonable speed and certainty have been described, and it has been pointed out that the best of systems of library arrangement can be spoilt by inaccurate shelving. Particularly in large libraries, with separate sequences of shelving for books of different sizes; with, perhaps, special collections of books shelved apart from the general stock; and with an abundance of material of odd sizes and shapes, correct shelving and filing is an essential. It is equally important that there should be good curatorship, or care of the stock. There is an unfortunate tendency on the part of some users of libraries to treat books very badly. Quite new books are sometimes returned after use in a shocking condition —with stitching forced apart, or cover damaged, or loose pages, or marks of greasy hands and fingers, or dog-eared corners of pages where these have been folded over to mark a place. Most libraries have a regulation which makes such damage an offence for which a fine can be charged, and there should be no hesitation in enforcing it, though this must only be done by a senior officer or by the librarian himself. Such abuse of the privilege which provides an almost unlimited range of books is happily not frequent, but it does occur; an unsocial act of this nature must needs be discouraged in every possible way, particularly in these days of book shortage and inferior paper and bindings.

The contemporary book production is doubtless the best that publishers can manage, but it is notable that the quality varies greatly between publisher and publisher. At their best, published books have a very limited life, at least, so far as lending libraries are concerned, before stitching and covers require treatment; indeed, the most that can be expected from books as published is about twenty to twenty-five issues or readings. After this they require to be rebound or recased, and a specially strong method of rebinding books for library use has been developed which gives much longer life than publishers' bindings (see Chapter XI). Rebound books may, with reasonable use, last for an additional seventy to one hundred issues, by which time both cover and pages are likely to be too soiled for any further use, though the stitching of the book may be as good as ever. It used to be the custom to cover rebound books in dark colours—cloth or leather, or a combination of the two—because these do not show dirt so readily as lighter coloured materials; but the drab appearance of long runs of books bound in black, or dark blue, or chocolate-brown, led to a campaign for brighter colours, which are now the rule rather than the exception.

Older books, particularly reference library or special collection stock, are more often to be found in leather bindings than in their original covers; and it should be remembered that the issue of books in wrappers or in paper boards, to be bound to suit the taste of individual owners, was formerly a common practice, and many of the books in decorated (gold-tooled) bindings, now to be found in libraries, were once in private collections. These older leather-bound books, especially those bound in calfskin, are a special problem as, in process of time and through change in atmospheric conditions, the leather, particularly on the spines of the books, becomes decayed, and powders on being touched. The only satisfactory solution to this problem is to rebind, or to repair by supplying new leather to the spines, which is very skilled work.

Problems of curatorship such as these should be matters receiving regular and systematic attention by senior members of the staff. But there are other matters (concerned with the daily routine of all who work in libraries and whose duties are mainly with the handling, shelving, charging and discharging of books), which should be an essential part of good librarianship. Books which need repair because of loose or torn pages, or damaged bindings, should be removed from the general stock for attention immediately such defects are noticed; a book should never be forced into a shelf already full, by squeezing it in, as the first volume to be taken from that shelf afterwards will probably receive damage, such as the tearing of the covering of its spine by the force that must be exerted in its removal; books should not be used as weights or to raise the height of seats; they should be dusted or vacuum-cleaned when necessary, which will vary according to whether they are much or little used; they should be handled with care, and the bindings should never be forced back in opening the books to read them, or for any other purpose—and this is especially necessary in the case of new books. It is the custom in all libraries in which readers are admitted to the shelves to have a daily 'shelf-sorting.' To be well done, this includes more than sorting or tidying. The first thing to be done is to check the order of the books on the shelves and correct it wherever necessary, and as the eye passes along each shelf in turn, a watch should be kept for books showing signs of damage, such as loose pages or torn bindings, which should be taken out for repair. The next thing to be done is to even up the numbers of books on the shelves, and at the same time to straighten each row of books by bringing the edges of the spine flush with the outer edge of the shelf. After a reasonable amount of practice this work can be done very quickly, and its regular performance gives the same well-kept appearance in a library as good housekeeping does in a house.

Everything possible must be done to keep dust and dirt out of a library. When floors need sweeping a good sweeping powder should be used to prevent the dust from rising. Where ventilation is dependent on opening windows, those farthest away from the road should be used whenever possible. On wet days sufficient doormats should be available near entrances, so that as little damp and dirt as possible is brought into the library on readers' footwear. Indeed, everything should be done to prevent unnecessary wear and tear, and to preserve both bookstock and furniture and fittings in the best condition. It should also be remembered that book-cases, card cabinets and other fittings need periodical attention. The most favoured wood for these is oak, with a light coloured and polished stain, which shows signs of handling after a period of use, and requires thorough cleaning and repolishing.

The repairing of books by members of a library staff should be strictly limited, as unskilful 'repair'—so-called

—can be very damaging. If a single loose page is all that requires attention this may be fastened in, but care should be taken to use a minimum of paste, to see that the edge of the paper to take the paste is entirely without folds or crinkles, and that it is eased into its exact place with a bone paper-folder, leaving no margin to overlap the adjoining pages. Paste is also used for such labels and pockets as may be necessary for the charging system of the library, and here again the minimum should be used.

The use made of book jackets varies. In some libraries they are all removed before the books are made available to readers, and are used to form part of book displays or posters. In other libraries they remain with the books, and are only removed when they become dirty and unsightly. Some libraries provide plain book jackets, made with a pocket at one end and the other end plain, to be folded over the back cover of the book, thus making the jacket adjustable for varying book sizes. Specially valuable books, particularly in reference libraries, may be provided with cellophane jackets, which are both decorative and protective.

Other forms of library stock need equal care. Much-used maps should be backed with calico. Sometimes they are rolled and kept in tubes; sometimes they are cut into sections before being mounted, and a small space is allowed between each of the section edges for folding. Prints and other illustrations should be mounted on standard size mounts of varying sizes,[1] and be kept either in dust-proof boxes (or Solander cases) or in vertical files. When there is any considerable stock of

---

[1] Useful sizes of mounts are $11\frac{3}{4}'' \times 10''$, $15'' \times 11\frac{1}{2}''$, $18'' \times 12\frac{1}{2}''$, $22'' \times 18''$, and $26'' \times 20''$.

large size maps, plan cases should be provided, similar to those to be found in an architect's office, in which the maps can be stored flat. Lantern slides should be kept in specially made slotted boxes; photographic negatives should be stored in stout envelopes, with a print of the negative pasted on the outside of the envelope. Gramophone records should be filed in envelope albums.

Revision of stock as part of the general plan of book selection has already been touched upon (see Chapter VII). To be satisfactorily carried out it must be organized with care. A suitable method in lending libraries [1] is to take one main part of the bookstock each year, and carry out a thorough survey, which will comprise: first, an examination of each book to check the use that has been made of it during the past three years; secondly, ascertaining which books have been superseded by new editions without this having been noticed in the routine book selection; thirdly, pruning the out-of-date. With regard to the first point, if books have been used but little or not at all for two or three years, the reason for this should be considered. It may be that the books are out-of-date, or unsuitable, or unattractive, or it may be that they have been overlooked. A decision must be made whether any such book should continue on the open shelves of the library, or in the library at all. If it is thought that any books have been overlooked, they can be brought to notice in some special display; if their period of effective service appears to be exhausted, it must be decided whether to place them in the reserve stock of the library, or to discard them. Superseded books should be removed from open shelves, and either

---

[1] Reference libraries seldom discard. Stock is kept up to date by systematic check of new publications and of subject bibliographies.

discarded, pending the buying of new editions or other works which are up-to-date and accurate; or, if retained in the library reserve stock, should have a note pasted inside the front cover of each regarding its deficiencies. It is always to be borne in mind that in lending libraries to circulate books containing matter which is out-of-date or inaccurate is a disservice of which no library should knowingly be guilty. Reference library requirements are different; often out-of-date works are required for historical purposes.

After thorough revision and pruning of the section of the stock selected for this treatment in any particular year has been completed, the section should be checked with the classification scheme in use by the library, and a note should be made of any subjects forming part of it which are either insufficiently represented or are not represented at all. A decision should then be made as to desirable additions of subject matter, which can be turned into particulars of books by reference to the appropriate subject bibliographies.

When revision of the general bookstock proceeds along these lines systematically, year by year, the library keeps its freshness and appeal. Where it is not done, and particularly when to this is added an insufficient flow of new books every year, the library slowly but surely loses its appeal and its effectiveness.

Library stocktaking used to be a regular yearly process and, when concerned with lending libraries, which are more subject to losses than reference libraries, whether they are public or college or university libraries, the whole of the books on loan were called in as from a given date. The library was then 'closed for stocktaking' for a period of a week or a fortnight or even as long as a month. Some college and university libraries still call in all loaned books at the end of term or session (though not necessarily for stocktaking purposes), but few public libraries now close for this purpose, or call in the whole of their bookstocks, as any benefit obtainable from such a course is considered to be more than counterbalanced by the very great inconvenience it brings to the reading public. Complete stocktaking of large libraries is a difficult, prolonged and involved process, though smaller libraries, for example, those with bookstock of 20,000 or under, may manage a yearly stocktaking: the larger libraries usually confine taking stock to one or two sections a year; and in some libraries there has not been any attempt to take stock for a number of years, owing to staff difficulties and shortage consequent on war with its attendant dislocation of the ordinary procedures.

Whether large or small libraries, stocktaking follows a general routine—a record of each book is ticked or date-stamped in some prearranged way as the book passes through the hands of the person conducting the stock check. The form of record varies. In some libraries the stock cards of books are used: these are arranged in card cabinets in the order in which the books are shelved, thus forming a shelf-register. As each book is found, the chosen mark is made on the card, and the cards for all books not found are separated from the remainder. When all books on the shelves of the library have been gone through, a check is then made of all books on loan, and the cards for these books receive the check mark. After this, a systematic check is made at all other points of the service where books or records of their location are to be found, for example, books withdrawn for repair or rebinding, those on extended loan to tutorial classes, or in reserve stock pools, or in any other place. The stock cards for all books found are separated from the remainder as the work proceeds, leaving a residue of cards for all books which neither have been found, nor of which the location is known. The check of shelves, of books on loan, and all other records is then repeated at intervals, which usually reduces the number of missing books, until searching brings no result whatever, and, at this stage, the cards of books not found reveal the extent of the losses since the last stocktaking was made.

Instead of the stock cards, some libraries use special stocktaking sheets, each sheet containing particulars of books either by the same author or with a common classification number, and with columns following the book details—author, title, accession number and class number—at the top of which the date of stocktaking is entered. As each book is found a tick is made in the appropriate column.

A rough and ready stocktaking check can be made by counting the books and book records of loan, etc. and comparing the total arrived at with the known total of library stock. This gives an indication of the extent of losses. The process is often referred to as the taking of a census of books.

CHAPTER XI

BOOKBINDING

THE craft of bookbinding is as old as books; and books are much older than printing, which dates only from the middle of the fifteenth century. Before that time books were inscribed by hand, usually on vellum or parchment, and though this does not soil or wear out so easily as paper, it was necessary, then as now, to make them convenient for handling, to protect the pages or scrolls from dust and dirt, and to provide a means of labelling them for ease of reference. These same purposes are those for which books are bound to-day.

The essentials of bindings are few but important. They must provide protection for the pages: they must effectively keep the pages in place and in their proper order; they must hold the pages tightly together, but allow complete flexibility of opening out at any point; they must have covers which are both durable and as light in weight as possible; and the outer covers must be of material that allows title-pieces or other particulars to be lettered on them clearly and legibly.

The first method used was to attach pages of vellum or paper edge to edge in one long sequence, and when the work was completed, to roll it up like a roll of wallpaper, and it was from this that we got our word 'volume,' which means 'roll.' This form was satisfactory for the purpose of reading the roll from beginning to end; but it was an awkward form if it came to be used for reference by consulting some particular short sequence of lines. From this, and for this and other reasons, the 'codex' form was developed, which is substantially the book form as we know it to-day. Instead of the pages being attached edge to edge, the sheets were folded across the middle, each sheet thus becoming two leaves or four pages. The next development was to fold the sheets, one inside the other, into what is now termed a 'gathering'; and from this form of gathering developed the system, which has been in common use for about five hundred years, of printing sheets in such a manner that, when folded, the pages fall into their correct order. From this manner of folding come the size-names of books—folio signifies that the sheets have been folded once only, forming two leaves; quarto, folded twice to make four leaves; octavo, folded three times to make eight leaves, and so on. These terms are still in common use, with adjectives attached such as post, demy and royal, which indicate the size in inches of the sheet before folding and consequently the page size; but as there is some variation in the size in inches of sheets with a common adjective, such as post, accuracy of description can only be obtained by stating the size of the book pages in inches or centimetres, which is a feature of extended cataloguing.

All books, then, consist of folded sheets, which in their folded form are known as 'sections.' It is the custom to number pages consecutively in order to give them identity, these numbers being usually printed at the outer top corner of each page; and it is the custom also to number the sections consecutively, generally by using the letters of the alphabet—the first section being marked A, the second B, and so on; letters I and V are not used, and if there are more than twenty-four sections the twenty fifth becomes AA, followed by BB, etc.—which usually appear at the left side of the bottom of the first page in each section. When the sheets come to the binder from the printer they are collated (that is checked for completeness), folded and stacked in piles according to section letters. A 'book' is formed by taking one of each of the sections, and bringing them together in their proper order; and when this is done, the 'book' is ready for sewing.

Most of the processes of making books are now performed by machines which do not exactly follow hand methods, but seek to achieve the same result; and only an expert can distinguish a machine-sewn book or a machine-cased book from one that has been done by hand. The various necessary processes are best studied from hand-sewn and bound books, and it is these that are described here.

Sewing of books is done by passing a thread—which should be of strong linen—through the folds of each book section in order to hold the pages in that section together. When section A has been sewn, the needle carrying the thread is then passed through section B, and so on. In order to hold the sewn sections together, and also to supply a method of holding the boards which form the cover of the book, the sewing is done over tapes, which lie across what becomes the spine of the book, and are usually given overlapping ends. Sewing is done with the help of a frame which has a base with two pillars, one at either end, and an adjustable crosspiece which lies parallel with the base at whatever height is desired within the limits of the height of the pillars. Lengths of tape of the required thickness are stretched between base and crosspiece, the number of tapes varying according to the size of the book to be sewn—usually three tapes to a crown 8vo, etc. The sewer begins by adjusting the tapes on the frame, then takes the first section of the book to be sewn, presses the folded back of this against the tapes, and then passes the threaded needle through the fold from the outside, leaving a thread end at the point of entry. She then sews through from the inner fold at the nearer end of the first tape, and in again at the other side of the tape, so that the thread passes over it. This process continues along the length of the fold until the thread has been passed over all the tapes, and then the needle is passed from the inside to the outside of the fold about an inch along. The next section of the book is then placed in its exact position above the first, and the needle is passed through the fold from the outside directly above the final point of issue in section one, and the sewing proceeds along section two, over the tapes as before. The needle is passed out of the second section immediately above the point of entry of the first section, where the loose thread has been left, and the loose end is now tied to the thread length. The third section is placed in position, and sewn over the tapes as before, and when the needle issues at the point an inch below the lowest tape, it is passed through the loop of thread joining sections one and two, and tied, this being called a 'kettlestitch.' Sections four and following are sewn in the same way as number three, with the kettlestitch at alternate ends as the sewing proceeds. When all the sections have been sewn, the book is taken from the sewing frame by cutting the tapes, leaving an overlap of tape at each side of about one inch. A paper sheet folded across is either pasted or sewn at beginning and end to form 'endpapers.'

Having been sewn, the book is now ready to be prepared for casing or binding, the difference being that if 'cased,' the whole of the back and sides of the cover are made in one piece as a separate process, and this case is attached to the book by means of the tapes; whereas in 'binding' the sides and back (or spine) of the book are attached separately.

Preparation for binding consists of strengthening the spine and giving it that rounded appearance so familiar to all who handle books. As the books come from the sewing-press, they are put into the guillotine or cutting-press, and all edges are trimmed off. The spines are then coated with glue, and when this is nearly dry, the binder lays each book on a solid surface and hammers the spine downwards and inwards, which rounds it. Next, each book is put into a backing-press, which has two flat cheeks, in such a way that the whole of the sides of the books are caught by the cheeks of the press, leaving the rounded back just above the level of the cheeks, against which are fitted wedge-shape boards with the thicker end nearest the spine. The press is then tightened, and the rounded back is hammered from the centre, outwards and downwards, which accentuates the roundness, and at the same time, assisted by the backing-boards, makes a groove between the spine and the sides of the book into which the board will fit.

On being taken from the backing-press, the spine is then strengthened still further by receiving another coating of glue, a layer of mull or muslin, and possibly one of strong paper also; and it is then ready for its cover.

If the cover is a 'casing' it will have been prepared, and all that remains is to attach the ends of the tapes to the inside of the boards of the case, and paste the endpapers to the insides of the boards. If the book is to be bound, the sides and the back are attached separately. First the tapes are attached to the boards which are to cover and protect the sides, either by being glued to the insides of the boards, or by being forced into a split made in the board itself. As 'boards' are either strawboard, or some stronger form of fibre boards made in layers, this matter of splitting them for the entry of the tapes can be done quite easily with a cobbler's knife; but sometimes the split is artificially prepared by glueing two boards together and leaving a small portion unglued.

When the sides or boards have been attached, there remains the covering to be done, the material used being either cloth or leather or a combination of the two. If cloth alone is to be used, a piece of the exact size necessary is cut out, and that portion of it which will cover the spine of the book is reinforced by having a strip of strong brown paper or millboard glued to it. When this has been done the cloth is coated with glue, except the reinforced part which will become the spine, and the corners are trimmed off. The closed book is then placed on the cloth, so that the inside edge of the board is in exact position in relation to the spine. The cloth is then stretched over the book, and the top cover smoothed down, then opened, and the overlapping cloth folded over and smoothed into position, a process then repeated for the other cover. To force in the fold of cloth at the top and bottom edges of the spine, it may be necessary to make a slight nick with the scissors through the mull or muslin covering the spine of the book.

When the cover has been stretched on, the outer endpaper of the book is pasted to the inside of the board, and this covers the folded over portions of the cloth. The book is then ready for 'finishing.'

Bookbinding is divided into two parts, 'forwarding' and 'finishing,' and the processes described up to the present are those included in the term 'forwarding.' If the cover is not to be cloth, but leather, the process is as described, in which case it will be known as leather bound. If the spine only is to be leather, and the sides cloth, the spine is dealt with first and the sides afterwards, a process known as quarter leather. If spine and corners are of leather, it is known as half-leather; and if spine and the whole of the front edges are of leather, this is called three-quarter leather bound. Where the covering of the spine is prepared as described, the book is said to have a 'hollow' back; if the covering is glued to the spine—a process carried out only with leather—the book is said to have a 'fast' back.

'Finishing' in binding comprises all lettering and embellishment on the outer covers. In most books bound for libraries this is confined to the lettering of particulars of author and title, class numbers, and possibly an occasional small ornamental panel or fillet. Sometimes valuable books for reference libraries receive more ornamental treatment, and the art of the bookbinder's finisher is well worthy of study. Specimens of decorative bookbinding are to be found in the showcases at the British Museum and elsewhere. Most of the decoration is called 'tooling,' because it is impressed by means of a heated binder's tool. If it is a simple impression it is known as 'blind tooling'; if the impression is made over gold leaf it is 'gold tooling.' Other decorations may include inlay work, when contrasting shades of leather are inserted or let into the main covering; sometimes there are centrepieces consisting of portrait miniatures, precious stones, and many other decorations. The art of the binder's finisher is of considerable variety and interest.

In addition to the straightforward work of binding, many books require expert repair from time to time. An instance of this is the time-decayed calf leather spine already referred to. Other instances are the need sometimes for fresh title-pieces, or for resewing an imperfectly sewn book. It is a great convenience when such work can be done on the library premises, and a few public libraries carry out the whole of their own binding work, having a special staff for the purpose. This is an economical possibility only where there is a need for the treatment of a minimum of 300 books a week, as less work than this is not sufficient to keep a well-balanced binding staff fully occupied.

The materials used in library binding—cloth, leather, strawboards, leatherboards, millboards, thread, mull, glue, paste, etc.—should be of the best quality obtainable. Inferior materials make for inferior work, and what is desirable is work of the most tasteful appearance, but of a quality and strength that will stand up to much, and sometimes unfair usage. Really well bound books will keep their shape, preserve their general appearance, and give service of duration and quality far above what may be obtained by using cheap materials and poor workmanship.

Manufacturers of bookbinding cloths make them in varying strengths, and often include in their range a specially strong cloth for library books. Besides this, there are ranges of buckram which are also well suited to withstand hard wear; and strong canvas is particularly useful for heavy works such as bound volumes of newspapers. The leather used in binding library books is usually Niger morocco, which comes from Nigerian goats. Pigskin used to be very much favoured, but is now too expensive for general use. Other leathers, such as calf, sheep and seal are in use—calf and sheepskin mainly for law books and ledgers; sealskin for private book-collectors, on books light in weight, when a specially smooth surface is required.

CHAPTER XII

MEMBERSHIP AND REGISTRATION

MEMBERSHIP of non-public libraries is usually limited to members of the society or institution to which the library belongs, e.g. the Library Association, the Royal Geographical Society, and the Royal Institute of British Architects. The libraries of universities and colleges are mainly for the use of students and staff. The libraries of government departments are mainly for the departments concerned. Few, if indeed any, libraries in corporate ownership will, however, refuse to admit the serious student to their shelves on satisfactory introduction: but as they exist for a special purpose, the calls of that purpose, whatever it may be, come first. Some years ago all libraries of standing were approached by the National Central Library (or the Central Library for Students, as it then was) to ascertain which of them were prepared to lend their books to other libraries, and the majority agreed. In return, many of them received a small money grant from the Carnegie United Kingdom Trust for structural alterations, or for any other requirement, and these libraries, under the general term 'outlier libraries,' are a most valuable part of the service provided by the National Central Library.

Membership of public libraries, town or county, is governed by the terms of the Public Libraries Acts, which state that residents in the area of the local government authority concerned must be permitted to use libraries, established by the authority under the Acts, free of charge. The Acts state also that non-residents may also be allowed to use the libraries either free or for payment. Unreasonable use of libraries is prevented by the placing of discretionary powers in the hands of local authorities, who are permitted to make rules to govern the use of the libraries.

The rules or regulations (not rules *and* regulations, as so commonly stated) adopted by library authorities should contain, among other things, carefully designed clauses setting out the qualifications and privileges of membership. It might be thought—and, indeed, is sometimes held—that library rules are an unnecessary affliction, and that a public library can be managed without them; that they are nothing but red tape, and life has far too much of this. It is to be remembered, however, that the books in public libraries are public property, and that the buildings in which they are housed, and the furniture and fittings in those buildings are public property also; and being so they must, on the one hand, be equally available to all, and on the other hand, be well cared for, and the use of them, for the sake of all concerned, must not be allowed to become abuse. This can only be done by making rules to guide those concerned with management to carry out their duties in a proper manner. There must be rules governing membership of the library, therefore, and they must be both precise and clear.

The normal qualification for membership is residence or, as it is usually phrased in library rules, persons whose names appear on the register of local government electors. With these the only formality required is a simple promise in writing to be bound by the rules of the library in force for the time being. It is also usual to require residents who are not local government electors to obtain a guarantor for their membership. Children attending schools in the area are required to obtain sometimes a guarantor, sometimes only a recommendation from their schoolteachers.

The whole question of obtaining guarantors is the subject of controversy and argument. Some say that guarantors are essential, otherwise book losses and infringement of rules will make orderly management an impossibility. Others say that guarantors are unnecessary (for all who are not still at school, at any rate), and that the personal undertaking of residents should be accepted whether they are voters or not, bona fides being established by the production of identity cards. For children attending school, it is the general feeling that a recommendation without any personal financial obligation on the part of the teacher should be accepted. Guarantors, where this is insisted upon, are usually bound in the sum of £2 to £5 for the obeying of the rules of the library by the persons they guarantee; and this is the part to which serious objection has been taken. It is a matter on which a ruling cannot be given. Custom supports the insistence on guarantors; but those who disagree with this, point out the fact that there may be good and bad customs, and to continue a bad custom is not good policy.

Another custom which is under question is that which limits membership (borrowing facilities) to the library of the town or county in which registered members reside. It is now held by some librarians that borrowers' membership cards for public libraries should be available for use in any public library in the country. It has been a custom for some considerable time to allow visitors to seaside resorts to use the local public library during their stay on production of membership cards from their home towns; and arrangement has been made between all the metropolitan public libraries, with one exception, to allow interchange of membership. In addition, a number of towns in the provinces have indicated their willingness to honour the library membership cards of other towns.

If all public library systems were on a reasonably even level, the claim for interchange of tickets would have more to support it than it has at the present time, when some towns or counties with an excellent library service are quite near to others with a very poor service. If interchange of tickets were generally accepted, it is reasonable to suppose that residents in the town with the poor service would make use of the near-by good service, which would throw a heavy burden on towns with a good service, and relieve the badly serviced towns, unfairly, of their obligation. This is one of the main reasons for advocating a national library service, made compulsory by a new Act of Parliament, and with obligatory standards and duties, supported by grants from the national exchequer.

The usual method of enrolment of borrowers is to have printed application forms which are filled in by prospective borrowers, and submitted to the staff counter for check. When found satisfactory, membership cards bearing the names of the borrowers are issued to them, and they use these cards on their visits to the library to borrow books. It used to be the general practice to have a ledger-form register of borrowers, ruled in columns to show number, date, name and address of borrower, and name and address of guarantor. This ledger is now seldom used, its place being taken by the filing in name order of the forms of application for membership which, for this purpose, are printed on cards of the same dimensions as catalogue cards—$5'' \times 3''$. Consecutive numbering of members is still practised in some places but, for the most part, this also has been discontinued. In order to keep a check of the number of applications for membership received, a summary of each day's applications and cancellations is kept.

The number of tickets each borrower is allowed to have varies. In some libraries, one general ticket, on which any book available for lending may be borrowed, and another on which novels may not be borrowed, but any other book may, are issued. In other libraries the allowance of general tickets may be two or more. Three tickets per borrower is a fair allowance but, for those engaged in some special work, such as research projects, there should be provision made in the rules to allow more liberal borrowing.

Readers' tickets are provided for use in lending libraries only; but it sometimes happens that a student may require, for some special purpose, a book of which the only copy is in the reference library. In such cases it is sometimes possible (and should, of course, be covered by the rules) to make special arrangements for reference library books to be borrowed for limited periods. Special loans include also mounted pictures or illustrations of different subjects, lantern slides, microfilms and other student material for which special provision is made; but the general medium of loan is the ordinary reader's ticket. It is the practice in some libraries to lend sets of plays to dramatic societies, but these require special rules and a special form of borrower's card.

It is a usual practice to limit the period of validity of readers' tickets, the period varying from one to three years; but the most usual period is two years. When the tickets expire, the persons concerned are required to re-register by filling in a new application form which is checked as for new members, and new tickets are issued. A few libraries do not call for re-registration, allowing membership to run on indefinitely; but the periodical check which re-registration implies is desirable as a safeguard on the bona fides of members. Tickets as issued are not transferable, being available for the sole use of the persons to whom they are issued. This is not by any means always honoured as, quite frequently, readers lend their tickets to other persons. It is necessary, therefore, to have a rule which clearly states that all readers are responsible for any books that may be borrowed on their tickets, in case a reader using borrowed tickets defaults.

The card register of borrowers is revised at three monthly intervals, when all expired application forms are removed; and every endeavour should be made to ensure that readers whose membership cards become out of date renew their membership by re-registering as soon as possible, but certainly within three months. The register, pruned in this way, is assumed to represent the current membership at any given time, but many persons register who either do not use the library at all, or use it very little, so that the 'live' membership of a library—the number of persons making regular use of it—may be, often is, considerably less than the current register of members shows. It is to be remembered also that many persons leave one town for another without cancelling their membership of the library; and still more change their residence without notifying this, in spite of the usual rule requiring it to be done.

Lending borrowers' cards to friends and failing to notify changes of address cause much difficulty sometimes in tracing the whereabouts of overdue books. Communications from the library may be returned marked 'not known,' or 'gone, left no address,' and when this happens in connection with members who are self-guarantors, little can be done. If there is a guarantor, he should be approached to find out whether he knows the present whereabouts of the defaulting borrower; if nothing can be done, the particulars of the default should be written across the application form of the person concerned, and the card should be left in its place even when time-expired. Should the same person again seek to register as a member, the previous default will come to light on filing his new application form, and he can then be compelled to make good the previous default or be barred from membership. This form of 'blacklist' should be carefully kept.

The most effective way of ascertaining the 'live' membership of a lending library is to take periodical censuses of the number of tickets in use and on which books are on loan. The census should be taken either twice or four times a year, in order to cover the different seasons—more reading is done in the winter than in the summer, for example. It is made by taking a count of the tickets, representing book loans, in the charging trays on selected days, and the numbers for the different census days are averaged. The final figure can be usefully compared with the total figure of membership as given by the register of borrowers.

In the small centres of county libraries registration of members is not rigidly practised, as the readers and library workers are all personally known to each other.

Reference libraries are open to all comers without any form of registration, though some require the signatures of all who enter. For this reason, and because good reference library facilities are not available at small libraries such as those of the smaller towns, and the branches of town and county library systems, those who use reference libraries are drawn from a fairly wide area which ignores town and county boundaries. In the McColvin report this point (among many others) is examined, and it is suggested that the regional nature of reference library work should be recognised by their being subsidised by the government through one of the departments of State—probably the Ministry of Education.

Procedure in connection with non-resident members varies. It is usual to allow free membership of public libraries to non-residents who are employed or attend school or college in the area of the local authority concerned, and to restrict subscription membership to those who have no connection whatever. Other places allow free membership only to residents and ratepayers. Subscriptions vary, but the usual range is from five to ten shillings a year; and, in systems where guarantors are required for all but local government electors, subscription members must obtain the signature of a guarantor on their application forms.

In many libraries using the guarantor system, it is possible to leave a deposit of money in lieu of obtaining the signature of a local government elector. The deposit may be ten shillings or £1, which is retained by the library during the period of membership of the depositor. It may be reclaimed on surrendering membership cards and ceasing to use the library, less any debt for fines or other penalties that may have been incurred.

CHAPTER XIII

BYE-LAWS AND REGULATIONS

In the *Oxford English Dictionary* a bye-law is defined as "A law or ordinance dealing with matters of local or internal regulation, made by a local authority . . . for the regulation of their dealings with the public." 'Regulation' is defined as "A rule prescribed for the management of some matter, or for the regulating of conduct; and 'rule' is defined as "A regulation framed or adopted by a corporate body . . . for governing its conduct and that of its members."

At first glance all three appear alike, and the likeness is true with regard to 'regulation' and 'rule' which, in practice, mean the same thing, and the two words should not be used together, as they are so frequently; only one or the other should be used. There is an essential difference, however, between a bye-law and a regulation, as a bye-law must have the approval of the appropriate government department before being put into force, and it is invariably accompanied by a money penalty for infringement, which can be enforced in a court of law. A regulation, on the other hand, is a local matter between the authority and the public, and though an authority might take a case arising from infringement of a regulation to court, the infliction of any penalty would be at the discretion of the magistrates.

The making of regulations for the government and control of non-public libraries is entirely a matter for the governing body; that for public libraries is covered by section 15, clause 2, of the Public Libraries Act, 1892,

which reads: "The library authority may . . . make regulations for the safety and use of every library, museum, gallery and school under their control, and for the admission of the public thereto." This main Public Libraries Act for England and Wales did not give power to make bye-laws, though the similar main Act for Scotland of 1887 covered the subject very fully in clause 22. For England and Wales, therefore, a special Act for bye-laws became necessary and was passed in 1901, and section 3 of this Act deals with the matter comprehensively as follows: "A library authority may make bye-laws for all or any of the following purposes relating to any library . . . under their control, that is to say:
- (a) for regulating the use of the same and of the contents thereof, and for protecting the same and the fittings, furniture and contents thereof from injury, destruction, or misuse;
- (b) for requiring from any person using the same any guarantee or security against the loss of or injury to any book or other article;
- (c) for enabling the officers and servants of the library authority to exclude or remove therefrom persons committing any offence against the Libraries Offences Act, 1898, or against the bye-laws."

This latter sub-clause, as will be seen, links to it the clauses of the 1898 Libraries Offences Act, which specifies the following offences:
1. Behaving in a disorderly manner.
2. Using violent, abusive or obscene language.
3. Betting and gambling.
4. After proper warning, persisting in remaining in the library beyond the hours fixed for closing.

All matters named in the 1898 and 1901 English Acts, and for Scotland in clause 22 of the 1887 Act may be the subject of bye-laws. Any other matters must be dealt with by making regulations. If a new public libraries Act is drafted, as seems likely, it would be well to extend the range of library offences which may be dealt with through bye-laws, for example, the payment of fines for overdue books, the replacement of lost books, and the use of libraries by infectious disease contacts.

An examination of a typical set of library bye-laws will show that the meaning of terms of importance is defined at the outset, to avoid any confusion or misconception. Thus, the term 'library' may be defined as meaning "any and every library or reading room and the several rooms, offices, passages, staircases, entrances and exits forming part thereof and adjacent thereto"; and the term 'book' may be defined as including "any and every book, periodical, newspaper, pamphlet, picture, print, photograph, map, chart, plan or manuscript, or any other article of a like nature forming part of the contents of the library." These definitions are important in order to prevent any legal submission in a prosecution that what is under dispute is not within the terms of the bye-laws.

Following such necessary definitions come the clauses stating what may not be done, under penalty of prosecution and fine, and these must be expressed in the Acts of Parliament which legalise the making of the bye-laws. They include clauses forbidding (a) audible conversation in those parts of the library where quiet is essential—reference libraries and reading rooms; (b) obstruction of members of the staff in carrying out their duties, or of members of the public in enjoying the facilities afforded by the library; (c) the bringing into the building of animals which may annoy, or vehicles which may cause obstruction; (d) smoking in the library; (e) damaging the books or furniture and fittings of the library; (f) causing annoyance to others through offensive uncleanliness; (g) eating or sleeping in the library; (h) giving false information as to name or address; (i) removing books from the library without proper authorisation.

After the clauses dealing with offences there follow those dealing with penalties—the amount of fine which may be levied, and the removal from the library of persons committing offences.

All of the foregoing matters come within the scope of the statutory provisions; but there are other matters which do not, and on which precise guidance is necessary for the benefit of both staff and readers. One such matter has already been dealt with in the previous chapter—that relating to qualifications and privileges of membership. Other matters usually included in regulations for the management of libraries are a definition of the extent of the responsibility of the librarian, particulars as to hours of opening of the library and its various departments, and a general clause relating to the maintenance of order, and enforcement of the regulations, which links them to the bye-laws.

The qualifications of readers and of their guarantors, the method of enrolment of members, and the number of membership cards allowed to each enrolled member should be clearly stated. This and other matters relating to membership generally have already been dealt with. The open shelf—or open access—method of work in lending libraries calls for special regulations, first to limit entrance to registered members, or at least to allow staff discretion in the case of non-members; secondly, to forbid if desired, the taking of satchels, bags, umbrellas or other specified articles into the library.

Other matters requiring regulations include the use of ink in reference libraries—usually forbidden, sometimes allowed on special tables—tracing and copying, duration of use of works such as directories or periodicals required at the same time by more than one person, reservation of required books, and any other matters of special local significance.

A set of model bye-laws is given as Appendix B (p. 331) of the Departmental Committee's *Report on Public Libraries in England and Wales,* 1927 (Cmd. 2868); and a draft code of regulations, compiled by the London and Home Counties Branch of the Library Association is given in the *Library Association Record,* 1928, pp. 206–8. These model codes are the result of careful thought and discussion by experienced persons, and offer valuable guidance to any libraries adopting codes or revising existing ones; but they should not be followed slavishly. It is most desirable that bye-laws and regulations should be framed so as to fit particular local circumstances, and it may be found necessary, for this purpose, to add to or to revise the model codes.

Bye-laws and regulations should not lightly be adopted, but when once this has been done they should be enforced. There is no need for such enforcement to be officious, in fact, officiousness in a library is most distinctly out of place and terribly irksome, but attendants on duty must have specific guidance if they are to do their job properly; and the library staff need guidance also as to what is and what is not permitted.

Without this, staff members, particularly the young and inexperienced, may tend to develop bad library habits, such as reserving books for friends, reading through periodicals or even books before putting them into circulation, or allowing novels to be borrowed on membership cards available only for non-novels. These actions, and any of a similar kind that tend to favour the few over the many, are thoroughly bad, as they become known and talked about—quite rightly—and lead to great dissatisfaction. They should be stamped out whenever and wherever found. A public library should have—and earn—a name for complete fairness of administration to all members alike. On the other hand, there are some rules which are still quite common, and rigidly enforced, which serve no useful purpose and only cause bad feeling and disdain. Such is the rule which requires a form of application for membership to be lodged two or three days or more before the applicant may use the library; and the rule that any book borrowed must be returned to the library from which it was borrowed, where there are several or many libraries in the same system; and the rule which requires an applicant to state his occupation; and the rule which requires members to pay for their membership cards, or for the forms of application for membership.

In all things library bye-laws and regulations should have as their essential basis the forwarding of the interests of members and of staff; they should be as few as possible; and they should be expressed in the simplest possible terms. They should also be widely publicised, so that all who use the library will know both their privileges as members and their obligations. It is useful to have a framed copy of bye-laws and regulations near the entrance doors, as this helps the hall attendant on the odd occasions when he has to deal with a difficult or obstinate person who persists in doing something—smoking in the building, for example—which is not allowed. All newly registered members should be given a copy of the regulations, and copies should be readily available at all service points.

Some librarians have compiled and circulated attractive leaflets on the contents and use of the libraries under their direction, and in them have embodied the substance of the library regulations in a simple and readable form. This is a useful practice well worthy of emulation. Another good practice is to print extracts from the regulations where they are likely to serve a useful purpose—on the date-labels of books, giving the details of duration of loans, and particulars of fines; on overdue notices sent out calling in books kept longer than the time allowed for reading them; on volumes containing scarce or valuable maps, dealing with particulars relating to making tracings. This should not be carried too far, and should be used only to protect the interests of readers and library alike.

CHAPTER XIV

ISSUE METHODS

A PRIVATE person, with a small library, may keep a check of any book borrowed from his shelves by leaving the empty space of the withdrawn book, and placing in it a slip bearing the name of the borrower, the title of the book, and the date when it was borrowed. This paper slip and the empty space give the owner all the information he needs about the transaction, and are a sufficient reminder to him to call in the loan whenever he may desire to do so.

Borrowing books from a library must be accompanied by a system which will give this information clearly for continuous series of transactions in quantities great and small. According to the size of the library there may be, at any one time, 50 or 50,000 books on loan, and each separate loan must be registered in such a way that the registration will disclose which copy of a book has been borrowed, when it was borrowed, and who borrowed it.

When libraries were in their infancy, the necessary details could be kept in a ruled ledger with columns for the required details of date, book and borrower. Later, when the numbers of borrowers increased, but before the institution of the open-access or open-shelf system, indicators containing columns of numbers in numerical order (fifty or one hundred to the column) were fitted to counters and designed to do two things: first, to tell borrowers whether a book with a given number was available for lending or not; secondly, to show when any book had been borrowed, and by whom, which was done by having a slot next to the number, or carrying the number, into which a reader's ticket could be inserted.

The indicator system was cumbrous and clumsy, and in no way suitable for work in open-shelf libraries, and even libraries which used it proceeded to discard it on changing over to the open-access system. Instead, they adopted a card index system which had been in process of development at the same time as the indicator system. The principle on which this card system is based is that each book is given a card, and each reader is also given a card. The book card contains written particulars of author, title, and distinguishing number of the book to which it belongs; the reader's card contains particulars of his name and address, together with other details required for routine purposes, such as date of issue and expiry of membership. When a book is borrowed, the book card and the reader's card are brought together, and filed behind a date guide of the day on which the transaction takes place, or on which the loan expires, according to the rules of the library. As it is desirable that the two cards should be joined in some way to prevent their becoming separated, and to facilitate the process of filing, either they are inserted in a small pocket, or one of the cards, usually that of the reader, is made in the form of a pocket into which the other will fit. Size and shape of tickets and pockets vary, but they are always made in such a way that, when joined together, the book number on the book card appears clearly at the top, and filing is by the book numbers. In a few libraries, arrangement is by classification number, which then appears at the top of the card in place of the book or accession number.

An adaptation of the ordinary card system is that known as the Dickman card charging system, used mostly in America, though at least one library in England uses, or has used it. The Dickman system provides each book with a card, but the reader's ticket is a metal tally, with a distinctive number appearing on it in relief. A machine is necessary for operating the system. When a book is borrowed, the book card and reader's tally are placed in the machine, and on pressing a lever the number on the tally is embossed on the book card, which is then filed in the ordinary way. The reader retains his tally, and so may come to the library at any time and borrow books without returning those he has on loan, as he must do in the ordinary system.

A new system which is still in the experimental stage is that of the punched card. With this, all processes of charging and sorting or filing are carried out by machinery. Each reader's name and each book are coded, and when a book is borrowed, the code particulars are tapped out on a keyboard resembling a typewriter keyboard, and a card bearing the coded details is discharged from the machine. Sorting is done by another machine, which can also abstract from a collection of cards, at incredible speed, any bearing any selected coded particulars, for example, all books on loan by authors whose names begin with the letter B; or all books borrowed on a given date, or in a given class. As a system it has most interesting possibilities, but its cost makes it prohibitive for the present.

Equipment and fittings necessary in working a book issue system include a desk or counter, card trays, date stamps and the cards for books and readers which have already been described. For small libraries or departments, such as junior libraries, a specially fitted desk may be found sufficient in place of the counter which is essential in larger libraries. Types of counter vary. Some are four- or three-sided, with a space for assistants in the middle. Some are circular, or horseshoe-shaped, again with staff space in the middle. Particularly for large libraries, either double or treble counters are necessary, or a long counter of the post-office type, which allows several persons to receive attention at the same time. Where double or treble counters are in use the counter work is divided into sections, usually according to selected sequences of days, each of the counters dealing with one of the chosen sequences. One counter, for example, might deal with books issued on March 1st to 8th, or on any date before March 1st; the second might deal with the period March 9th to 12th, and the third March 13th to 15th. A major difficulty with multiple counters is that a person might be returning at one time books borrowed on different dates, which would entail his attendance at more than one place to discharge them.

An interesting development of the long counter is to make it face inwards instead of outwards. By the ordinary counter routine, borrowers visiting the library to exchange their books proceed first to obtain a discharge for the books they are returning, and then pass into the library to choose others. Where the counter faces inwards, borrowers pass straight into the library, thus avoiding any necessity to queue. When inside the library they arrange the discharge of the books they have on loan either at once or later. In theory this system is supposed to prevent queues, but at busy times these form inside the library instead of outside, as in other libraries with the counter facing outwards. A further arrangement is to have the book-discharge counter in a hall by itself, outside the lending department.

Whatever the type of counter, it should be fitted with a raised shelf or ledge on the side used by borrowers—a ledge on which they place the books they are returning for staff attention. Sometimes these shelves or ledges are flat, and parallel with the counter top; sometimes they are sloped downwards and inwards, so that books placed on them lie at an angle of about 45°, and are in the line of sight of a person looking downwards from inside the counter. The counter top should be about 2' to 2' 6" deep, and on that portion used for discharging book loans lie the trays containing the book charges. It is a convenience to arrange these trays at an angle, sloping slightly downwards away from the staff side of the counter, which is made possible by having a low step on the counter top on the staff side. The book charges are the joined readers' cards and book cards filed behind date guides in shallow trays usually about 18" to 2' long, the inside width being about ¼" greater than the book charges they hold, so that these can be moved freely and easily. A greater length of counter space is needed for discharging loans than for charging out newly borrowed books, although in the four- and three-sided counter the same space is allowed for both purposes. Where the long counter is in use it is sometimes fitted with a return at right angles to the main length—the shape of a capital L—and books are stamped and issued on this extension.

When the open-access system was first developed by James Duff Brown it was called safe-guarded open-access, because to the counter were fitted two self-locking wicket gates, the latches of which could be operated only by the staff inside the counter. No one could either enter or leave the library unless a member of the staff released the latch of the appropriate gate. Wicket gates of this type are still used, but sometimes a form of turnstile has been substituted. In many libraries it is used more as a guard in the temporary absence of staff on counter duty than as a regular feature of the service; and in some libraries there are no guards at all on entrance or exit. The great majority of those who use public libraries do not need rigid supervision on their movements; and the few who do would find a way to defeat the guard imposed by wicket gates if they chose to do so.

Card systems of book issue are usual, and they are of two kinds—book card in tray, and book card in book. The first of these is seldom used. With it all book cards are arranged in numerical order in trays at the book-issue part of the counter. When a borrower brings to this counter a book he has obtained from the shelves and wishes to borrow, the assistant finds the number given in the book, and then obtains the appropriate book card from one of the trays. An advantage of this system is said to be that it acts as an indicator of books on the shelves, but its use wastes much staff time. The other system—book card in book—requires each book to have a pocket pasted in it (usually inside the front board) to hold the book card. Whatever system of book issue may be used, it is necessary that each book should have in it a record that will direct the assistant to the place where the charge of book card and reader's card is to be found, and the usual method is to paste a date-label on the front fly-leaf of each book and, at the time of issuing the book, to stamp on this label either the current date or the date when the loan expires—the latest date on which it may be returned without incurring a fine. The best type of date-stamp for this purpose is the self-inking metal one; but whatever type is used, the impression should be clearly legible, and neatly placed on the date-label—by no means always found on looking through the date labels when visiting libraries. As the day's work at the issue counter in a library proceeds, the charges of books issued that day go on increasing, and at the end of the day they will require sorting into the order adopted for the system to which they belong. Some libraries arrange charges of books on loan by the accession numbers of the books; some by classification numbers, books in the same class being subdivided in alphabetical order of author's names. The former insures the greater speed in discharging loans at the returns counter; the latter, though it slows down routine work, gives important information more readily—for example, the whereabouts of any book on loan at a given time, or the number of books on loan at any given time in any special subject, such as electrical engineering or psychology. The method adopted is a matter for local choice.

The lending of collections of books to tutorial classes, and loans to other libraries through the machinery of the regional library bureaux and the National Central Library, calls for special methods. Bulk loans are usually for an extended period of three months or more, and the book cards should be filed in order behind a place-and-date-guide apart from the general charging trays. Regional library bureaux loans may either be registered in a ledger or in a card index system, also apart from the general charging trays. Place and date guides are necessary for them also.

The charging or book-issue section of lending library counters is usually fitted with card-sorting compartments of one kind or another. Each compartment is labelled with a block of numbers—either book accession numbers or classification numbers—and as books are charged out to readers, the charge is placed in the compartment to which the book number belongs. At the end of the day this partial sorting assists greatly in the final arranging in order of the charges before their transfer, behind the relevant date-guide, to the charging trays of the returns section of the counter.

Usually the trays of book-charges at the returns counter are arranged in a line, but an interesting recent development is to arrange them round a turn-table which, on releasing a catch, will spin round to bring any wanted tray to the hands of a seated assistant. The ordinary straight line of trays is sometimes laid on a railway, and may be moved as a whole, left or right, to bring any wanted tray to the hands of a seated assistant.

Probably ninety per cent of books borrowed by readers are returned within the time allowed for reading them. Many of the remaining books are returned within two weeks after the dates on which they are due for return, and it is usual to charge a small fine for books kept longer than the allowed period—overdues, as they are called. If they are not returned within this time notices are sent to the readers concerned—overdue notices—which call for the return of the books, and notify the reader of the amount of the fine that has been incurred, to which it is usual to add the cost of sending the notice. If no reply is received, a further notice is sent to the reader a week later. This is followed, where necessary, by a letter to the guarantor, when the reader is not a self-guarantor.

Even after two or three such applications there usually remains a small number of outstanding cases which require further treatment. Some libraries send a messenger to the houses of readers, who may obtain the books, but seldom obtains the fines also; and in such cases the amount of the unpaid fine is entered against the reader concerned.

Beyond this stage in obtaining the return of overdue books, practice varies; but as a matter of principle, everything possible should be done to obtain the return of books. A system adopted in some libraries which has had a very marked success is to call on the assistance of the borough or city treasurer. With the help of the treasurer's department, an official bill, in the same form as a rate demand note, is sent to the reader for the cost of the book and the amount of the fine incurred. A copy of this bill goes to the treasurer, and is taken up by his collectors, who are widely experienced in tracing defaulters. With this help, the return of all but a very small portion of overdues is assured; and when the treasurer's collectors do not succeed, the outstanding bill, as a debt to the council, goes forward to the town clerk's department to be considered as a case for bringing suit in the county court. Two courses are then open, to sue either for both the value of the book and the amount of the fine incurred, or simply for the value of the book. The latter course is likely to be chosen, in the absence of power to make a bye-law relating to the charging of fines for keeping books beyond the time allowed in the library regulations for reading them, particularly as it is possible to find a case of a book valued at half-a-crown with a fine incurred of several pounds. At present we have no really satisfactory way of dealing with this question, which should be included for consideration when a new public libraries bill is being drafted.

Although the systems of book issue described have been related mainly to public library practice, the same principles cover the lending of books from any type of library, and are capable of adaptation to any special requirements.

CHAPTER XV

REFERENCE LIBRARIES: MATERIAL AND METHOD

An experienced English librarian could readily name many works he would expect to find in any British reference library. These would be the well-known publications that are the backbone of reference library work, books in general and everyday use containing, as they do, the answers to thousands of questions that arise again and again—the time of a train, the meaning of a word, the address of a business house or professional man, the holder of a public office, the population or market day of a town, and so on. The books which provide answers to such questions include the standard encyclopædias, dictionaries, directories, time-tables, almanacs and yearbooks. They are essentially works to be referred to for special factual information, and the form in which they are compiled is designed to simplify to the greatest possible degree the task of making use of them. In all of them the order of the letters of the alphabet is widely used, as it is assumed that every one is familiar with this; accordingly in many, as in general encyclopædias, the articles are arranged in alphabetical order; others, arranged in subject sections, are provided with alphabetical subject and topic indexes, giving page references where the relevant information may be found.

Development beyond this point should be systematic, but in practice this is not always found. Particularly in the past, there has been a tendency to treat the reference library as a museum or a safeguard—a museum for donated collections, sometimes presented with a proviso that they are to be kept together as a collection, possibly with a nameplate; as a safeguard, because to the reference library have been assigned all works costing more than a settled sum, £1 or some other arbitrary amount; or all works above a certain size, say large quarto; or all works on the fine arts with full-page plates. This does not make a reference library, but a show-place; and the very limited use that libraries of this kind receive makes them very expensive show-places.

Quite different should be the method of building up reference library material. Assuming that the outstanding reference works referred to above have been acquired, the next requirement is to build up the main subject classes with the works of reference relating to these subjects. Biography, for example, is a very important reference library subject, because it deals not only with the lives of men and women, but also with the parts played by them in the subject or subjects which formed their life work. The student of the history of music, for example, will be required to know the part played by Beethoven, Purcell, Elgar, and many others; the student of literature the interrelation of life and work of Chaucer, Milton and others; and similarly with other subjects. Biography, then, as a reference library subject is pervasive, and must be represented by dictionaries of biography, national and universal, of which there are many.

Other subjects need similar treatment in order to include sufficient material for their adequate representation. For religion there are the dictionaries of Hastings for the Christian religion, as well as concordances of the

Bible, and also dictionaries of non-Christian religions, and of mythology, which is related to early forms of religious beliefs. There are dictionaries of chemistry, of physics, of medicine, of history, of sociology, of music; and for most broad divisions of knowledge; and for most subjects, and many divisions of subjects, there are available bibliographies of varying worth, some excellent, some not so good. For librarians working in this field of book selection there are two essential bibliographies which should be known and used by all of them—these are Isidore Mudge's *Guide to Reference Books* (and supplements), and Minto's *Reference Books* (with supplement). The first of these is American in origin, and has some American bias, but is of the utmost importance in the English-speaking world; the second is of equal importance, but is now out-of-date and requires revision, which it is now receiving from the Publications Committee of the Library Association.

Mudge and Minto deal not only with books that are essentially works of reference, but also with standard texts, which are the next broad class of books that should be in the stock of a reference library. Some of these are more used for reference purposes than for continuous reading, e.g. the *Cambridge Ancient, Medieval* and *Modern Histories*, and the *Cambridge History of English Literature*. Others are the books of standard authors whose work is a quarry for all later workers in the same field—Plato, Marx, Gibbon, Darwin and many others; and the serial publications of learned societies, such as the Surtees (history, particularly ecclesiastical); Harleian (history and genealogy), Walpole (art history), and those of local historical, antiquarian and scientific societies.

The next broad class of material is that emanating from the State and its various departments, known usually as government publications. These are so many and so varied in subject matter that a guide to them is essential, and is published by H.M.S.O., revised at frequent intervals from daily lists of publications also circulated by H.M.S.O. Government publications range from the volumes issued at intervals by the Historical Manuscripts Commission, through the reports of Royal Commissions and Departmental Committees on special subjects of national importance—e.g. the reports of the various commissions dealing with the mining and marketing of coal, and the report of the Departmental Committee on public libraries in England and Wales—to the order papers of the current sittings of the Houses of Parliament, and the daily report of proceedings in the two Houses, colloquially known as Hansard, from the name of its first editor.

Serial publications of value in reference libraries include not only bound and indexed files of weekly, monthly and quarterly journals, such as the *Architect*, the *Connoisseur*, the *Illustrated London News*, *Notes and Queries*, and the *Library Association Record*, but also the published transactions of societies such as the English Association, the Thoroton Society of Nottinghamshire, and ASLIB (Association of Special Libraries and Information Bureaux). Some societies publish valuable abstracts of articles and theses culled from international sources and in a variety of languages, e.g. the Abstracts of the Chemical Society.

Libraries in industrial and business areas make special provision for local commercial reference requirements, and sometimes, in the larger cities, these are accorded a special department known as the commercial library, which may be in the Central Library or elsewhere. The material required is an extension of the business section of general reference libraries built round local needs of manufacturing and marketing. Business directories of all parts of the world are to be found here, together with telegraphic codes, government marketing regulations, export and import details, transport by land, sea and air, dictionaries of commercial terms and their foreign equivalents in a variety of languages, trade periodicals, chamber of commerce bulletins, atlases; and in addition, fugitive material, frequently pruned, consisting of trade catalogues, which are particularly useful for the illustrations they contain, and clippings from newspapers and periodicals, house journals, and even correspondence with business houses dealing with special questions and not of a confidential nature.

Beyond this stage there is no limit to the books and other material which a reference library may collect with profit, and no one can tell when or for what reason any part of it may be wanted. Having covered (as all reference libraries should, to be worthy of the name) the field of general inquiry, and represented each main subject division by including both its particular works of reference and its basic texts, the broad field of general literature is entered, and many books may be acquired, each giving additional strength to the section of which it forms a part. Many such works may already be included in the lending or home reading department of the library, but that should not deter the adding of them to the reference library; moreover, in reference libraries, large or small, it should be possible to call on lending or home reading library material to supplement the reference library's own resources; and when a reference library reaches the size where textbooks form part of its normal stock, it should be made possible to lend them for limited periods to persons or to other libraries if this can be done without inconvenience. The lending out of reference material, however, should be a matter left to the complete discretion of the librarian of the department.

To have the necessary stock is only one of several essential features of a reference library, the others being the satisfactory arrangement of the material, its adequate cataloguing, and staff work. Each is important, but staff work most of all. Few reference libraries can find room for all their stock in the public room containing the desks or tables for use by readers, and much thought has been given to the planning of bookstores—called 'stacks'— to house them. For most libraries, that is to say, for libraries serving a population of less than 200,000, rooms adjacent to the public room are the most convenient. In large libraries, particularly those built during the last twenty-five years, the reference library stack is an important feature of the building. It is usually vertical, that is, in the form of a tower, with floors every 6' or 7', all completely fitted with steel shelving with gangways of 3' 6" to 4', and the steel framework of the tower supports both the tiers of shelving and the intermediate floors, which are served both by a stairway and by at least one electric lift. Sometimes the stack is horizontal, that is, it runs over the whole of one or more floors of the entire area of the building. Whatever the type, and this applies to all reference libraries with whatever form of book storage they may be fitted, there must be a satisfactory routine process of obtaining required books with the least possible delay.

Usually reference libraries are classified on one of the recognised systems of book classification, but this is not invariable, and even where it is to be found, account must be taken of the fact that books in reference libraries vary greatly in size, from the small duodecimo to the large elephant folio, and shelving is usually in at least three sizes, known as parallel shelving. In addition, separate sequences are required for pamphlets and papers, for prints and photographs, which may be filed in boxes, or vertical files, or plan cases. Further, there is usually at least one special collection shelved separately —the local collection—and there may be several. The catalogue of a reference library, therefore, must not only give the usual author and subject information, but also clear indication of the exact location of each item.

It has already been stated that reference library cataloguing must be done very fully, as it must indicate the exact nature of the item, and as far as possible the extent of its contribution to the subject with which it deals, and its location in the library. The ordinary classification schemes may be used with good effect on the whole, but they will be found inadequate for special local material, and possibly for special collections, for which local arrangements must be made. These should follow the same process of reasoning that created the classification scheme of the Library of Congress, which was planned, subject by subject, to suit the material with which it was called upon to deal. It is a similar process of reasoning that appears to inform Dr. E. A. Savage's theory that the grouping of books by subject matter is more important than exact subject classification of books which, he suggests, is neither possible nor necessary. The subject grouping of books in some divisions in the special collections in Edinburgh Public Libraries, themselves a development of the similar groupings to be found in some American libraries, provides a demonstration of what is possible; but it has also the dangers of specialisation, and emphasis on the special at the expense of the general which, in library method, has obvious drawbacks, as many books would be claimed by more than one grouping, and, if carried out to its full extent, it would lead to unnecessary duplication. There is much to be said on both sides, however, and the works of Dr. Savage, of Miss Grace Kelly and others require careful attention.

Staff work in a reference library is of major importance, as the collections need interpretation and exploitation if they are to provide for readers their full resources. Many who use a reference library do so to find simple factual information readily obtainable from the essential reference books on open shelves; some need assistance even with these. But it is the enquiries for information, sometimes apparently simple, which tax the capacity of staff work: such enquiries, for example, as the mental outlook of the blind person; the identity and work of Sylvanus; the preservation of manuscripts; the functions and powers of the Assistance Board; trade marks of men's clothing; the storing of ammunition and explosives; the history of lighting. These, which are actual examples, and hundreds of others are answered every day in the reference libraries of the country, and mainly their answering, well or badly, quickly or slowly, depends on the resources of the library and the ability of the staff to use them. There are certain short cuts which may sometimes be taken, e.g. the use of the index volume of the *Encyclopædia Britannica,* and the index and text of Keesing's *Contemporary Archives* and of *Whitaker's Almanack*, but many enquiries demand much more than this: first, the reducing of the enquiry to its simplest and clearest form; then the obtaining of such information as may be gleaned from the general knowledge books, such as encyclopædias; then the use of subject bibliographies, and references in works consulted to other works; until there is gathered together a body of information which may be submitted to the searcher, and may produce what he requires, or lead to further searching. Experience in using books and in answering enquiries has a cumulative value, as it serves to relate one problem with another; and a subject index of questions, with the sources of information produced, if kept systematically, is frequently a time-saver. Many enquiries come by letter or telephone and, when possible, they should be answered immediately. Enquiries by letter may come from other libraries, particularly for local historical or biographical detail, possibly to be found only in local archives or manuscripts which it may be impossible to lend outside the building. In such circumstances, use is often made now of special photographic developments, such as the photostat and the microfilm. The former photographs directly on to sensitised paper, either to the size of the original or, within limits, reduced or enlarged, and it has the great advantage of enabling the actual material to be supplied in facsimile instead of a typed or hand-written copy. To students doing research work with original source material this is particularly useful, as they are able to note any corrections or alterations, as well as the nature of the script itself; and it prevents the possibility of mistakes being made in copying. Microfilm has similar advantages of reproducing original material, but is only used for work covering a number of sheets in continuous order, such as a manuscript account book, a record of proceedings of a council or committee, or an author's manuscript of an original work. It is produced usually on 35 mm. film, and needs a special magnifying apparatus to enable it to be read. These photographic developments are not yet widely employed, but their use is extending steadily.

The field of knowledge as contained in books is so vast that, however large a reference library may be, enquiries will be received for which the answer must be sought elsewhere. This problem has no satisfactory solution, but the London reference libraries are practising co-operation on original lines. Each is specialising in one main subject, and when enquiries are received outside the scope of the library receiving them, they are transferred to the library of which this subject is the speciality. Co-operation along these lines might be helpful if developed on a wider scale.

CHAPTER XVI

CO-OPERATION—REGIONAL AND NATIONAL

CO-OPERATION among librarians through interchange of ideas and the lending of books from one library to another has been a common practice for generations, but organised schemes of co-operation are one of the many developments in librarianship which date from the end of the first world war. The main schemes are regional or national in scope, but there were several of a purely local character—e.g. one in Nottinghamshire and another in East Anglia—in which groups of libraries within reasonable telephone distance agreed to lend books to each other as required, and also to keep each other informed of additions to stock, excepting for novels. Most of these have now been absorbed into the larger regional systems.

The main stream of development of co-operation has been through the still growing activities of the National Central Library. This Library, now of more than national importance, began in a small way as an agency for lending collections of books to adult education classes, such as those organised by the W.E.A.; and its early name was the Central Library for Students. It was created and developed by Dr. Albert Mansbridge.

During the period of early development of the county library service, between the years 1920 and 1925, difficulties were experienced in providing for the special needs of students in rural areas who wished to make use of the service, but whose requirements were books with low issue value, and often of high price, and sometimes scarce and difficult to obtain. The Carnegie United Kingdom Trust, whose benefactions were the responsible feature of the development and progress of county libraries, gave careful attention to this important problem and, as a result, an arrangement was made with the Central Library for Students to lend books for special needs to county libraries as required; but there were certain stipulations made so that the service would be used only for such special cases as would not fall within the ordinary and reasonable scope of any county library concerned. The main stipulations made were that only non-fiction books could be borrowed from the Central Library for Students, and their published price must not be below six shillings (later raised to ten shillings). In actual fact, the stipulations made were not always successful in their object, as there was a good deal of book borrowing that should have been book buying, but this was part of the parsimonious attitude towards county library expenditure found in many counties in their early years of development, which in most, happily, has now been thoroughly overcome.

Progress in the system of national lending of wanted books by the Central Library for Students was steady, and met with general approval, and the next stage of development took into account two things: first, that to meet all calls made on the system was beyond the reasonable expenditure of one library in buying required books, even with a subvention of respectable size; secondly, that in the country there are many specialist libraries, with large and valuable specialised bookstocks that are not by any means used to capacity, and that if these libraries would agree to lend books outside the borders of their own organisations, here was an incomparably rich pool on which to draw. This was tactfully explored, with considerable success. The Carnegie United Kingdom Trust offered financial assistance to many specialist libraries to pay for schemes of development, or for other purposes, on condition that these libraries would agree to lend books from their stock to other libraries, at the request of the Central Library for Students.

By this time many urban library systems had entered into the scheme of the Central Library for Students and, together with the county libraries, were subscribing to its funds, and making use of the system of borrowing; and year by year the number of special libraries willing to lend books increased, and many urban and county public libraries also volunteered to lend books to other libraries when requested to do so by the Central Library for Students. These libraries which entered into agreements with the Central Library for Students became known as outlier libraries.

Steadily, year by year, the work of the Central Library for Students increased, and in addition to its service as an agency for the supply of collections of books to tutorial classes, and the constantly growing number of books for which loan was requested, another activity was found necessary, namely, the supplying of bibliographical information—information on books and subject matter in libraries at home and abroad, which often led to requests for the loan of the material indicated or for part of it.

By 1930 the work had assumed importance on a national scale, and the Central Library received for the first time a grant from the Treasury; its title was now changed to the National Central Library. In the following year it was granted a royal charter. Up to this time the accommodation of the Library—offices and bookstores—had passed through a variety of makeshifts of growing size but little dignity, and the Carnegie United Kingdom Trust decided to bestow on the Library a suitable home. The time coincided with that of a similar need on the part of the Library Association for suitable headquarters, and the Trust decided to help with this also. The result was the building of Chaucer House and the adjacent National Central Library in Malet Place, with spacious and adequately functional interior planning, and quiet dignified exterior. The official opening was carried out by H.M. King George V in November, 1933—a recognition of the importance of the occasion.

By this time the number of public libraries that had agreed to lend books to other libraries through the medium of the National Central Library had increased very much, and was distributed over the whole of the country. This led to the development of the idea of regionalisation of schemes, which then received attention. It had been found in the work done by the National Central Library that an essential need to effective schemes of co-operation was the assembling of bibliographical information at a central point, and the building up of a union catalogue of outlier libraries was in progress at the National Central Library, an important part of which was the creation of the union catalogue of the Metropolitan public libraries, housed from its inception at the National Central Library headquarters. The idea was then conceived that much of the work which passed through the loans department of the

National Central Library could be decentralised and done equally well from regional centres, each of which would carry out its work on the same lines as those used in the National Central Library; but the work at each regional headquarters would be confined to the libraries situated in its own region. Each would have its own headquarters staff, and union catalogue of the libraries in its area, and each would arrange for the interlending of books by and to the libraries situated in the region. It was felt that probably about three-quarters of the book loans desired could be met in this way, and the remainder of the loan requests which could not be met locally would be dispatched to the headquarters of the National Central Library, in order to make use of the wider resources to which it had access. This, it was thought, would have three results. First, it would be quicker; secondly, it would greatly lessen the overburdened headquarters work of the National Central Library; thirdly, it would distribute the cost of the system over the whole of the country.

The suggestion to form a regional grouping in this way, the separate parts to be known as regional library bureaux, was put forward at meetings, and by correspondence with authorities and with the Library Association and its branches, by the Librarian of the National Central Library, and found much support, particularly as the cost of instituting regional schemes and the preparation of union catalogues was guaranteed by the Carnegie United Kingdom Trust. The country was divided into areas, each centring in one of the large public library systems, and meetings were called in each area so that local regional committees could be appointed to organise and direct the work. When these committees began their work, their first tasks were to form an estimate of the approximate size of the union catalogue for the area, the time and cost of its production, the form it was to take—card or sheaf catalogue—the staff necessary, and the arranging of the required accommodation. Regional library bureaux in this form began to be organised about the year 1931, and in the years since then they have become an active and important part of public library work.

Many universities and university colleges belong to the regional bureau in their area, but they have also a system of their own operating over the whole country and known as the Joint Standing Committee on Library Co-operation, the enquiry office of which is at the National Central Library. It was conceived and organised by the Association of University Teachers.

Although the principle of operating with a union catalogue as the focal point is the general one, the regional bureau of Yorkshire operates differently, on what is called a 'zonal' system. The area is divided into four zones, each centring in one of the large city libraries—Leeds, Sheffield, Hull and Bradford. When books are required, particulars are sent to the zone headquarters library, and when this library cannot lend, the other libraries in the zone are first applied to, and then, lacking success, the applications are forwarded in turn to the other zones. Applications that cannot be satisfied in any of the four zones are sent to the National Central Library. As there is no central headquarters or paid staff with this system, cost of maintenance is much less than in the other regions, and it is preferred there, though not generally.

The regional library bureaux make it known in all

libraries that an agency exists for obtaining the loan of books not in their own stock, and readers are invited to make their needs known. When a library desires to borrow a book through the regional library bureau to which it belongs, a form, supplied by the bureau, is filled in giving the bibliographical particulars of the wanted book, and the name of the library requiring it, and this form is sent to the editor of the bureau. Here it is checked with the union catalogue to find out which, if any, libraries in the area possess the book and, if only one has it, the form is sent to that library, which sends the book to the library requiring it; or, if it is not possible to lend the book, the form is returned to the bureau headquarters, which will then forward it to the National Central Library. If more than one library in the bureau area has the wanted book, each is asked in turn until the loan is arranged, or until it becomes necessary to seek the aid of the National Central Library. Books required by county libraries are sent direct to the reader instead of to the library. They are usually lent for one month, and each library keeps a register of books lent and borrowed which is checked daily to ensure the regular return of books either borrowed from or lent to other libraries. Overdue books are called in by a similar method to that used for the ordinary lending library routine.

The initial cost of establishing the regional bureaux and preparing the union catalogues was, as explained, financed entirely by the Carnegie United Kingdom Trust, but, as with all Trust activities, a time limit for maintenance cost was fixed, and at the end of this it became necessary to arrange for the bureaux to be financed by those using them. Many of the regional bureaux councils adopted a system of graduated subscription for the libraries in their areas, the smallest co-operating libraries paying a minimum yearly subscription, and this being increased by stages, according to local population, to a maximum subscription for the largest libraries—those serving a population above a certain figure, say 250,000. The executive committees of the regional library bureaux councils manage affairs, in similar manner to that of library committees, and they have executive powers delegated to them by the regional library bureaux councils. Each bureau has an honorary secretary who is responsible for calling meetings and taking minutes, and an honorary treasurer who looks after the finances of the bureau. The day-to-day work is carried on by a paid staff, the chief of which is usually called the editor of the bureau, although director is a better name and is coming into use.

The cost of postage was, in the early days of the movement, charged to the persons on whose behalf the loans of books were arranged, and this still applies in some libraries. An early development was that some libraries agreed to meet the charges for books borrowed for their own readers, but required postage on books lent by them to other libraries to be refunded. This has now changed in many libraries, which pay all charges on books they borrow and those they lend.

The contributions, both in money and service, are not even as regards small and large libraries. The large libraries, as a rule, lend much more often than they borrow, and their subscription to bureau funds is higher. It is felt, however, that the larger libraries should be prepared to make this contribution to the library system of the country as a whole and, though there are occasional grumblings, the book service from National Central

Library and bureaux is very highly valued. It is felt by some of the regional library bureaux committees, however, that, as the service is national in scope and centres in the National Central Library, it would be logical for the whole of the organisation to be governed and financed by the National Central Library and not by regional subscriptions, though regional committees, to settle local matters and to act as agents for the governing body of the National Central Library, would still be required. To meet the considerable increase in expenditure of the National Central Library which this would entail would require for it a very much expanded income, but it is thought that this would be a proper charge on the national Treasury. The National Central Library already receives a grant from the Treasury, which sum forms the major part of its yearly income, and the extension of this to meet the whole of the cost of the interloan of book service throughout the country is logical and appropriate. This matter is under consideration by the National Committee on Regional Library Co-operation, on which all the bureaux are represented.

The position in Scotland is complicated by the fact that the wording of the Scottish Library Acts has been ruled to be framed in a manner which makes it illegal for a public library in Scotland to lend its books to any other library, and because of this, regional bureau affairs in that country have been much delayed. A scheme to help Scotland was instituted and financed by the Carnegie United Kingdom Trust, and operated from the Trust headquarters in Dunfermline, working on the same lines as the National Central Library, but on a restricted scale. A way out has been found, and since 1946 a bureau for Scotland has been instituted on the English pattern.

The Carnegie United Kingdom Trust financed also the Irish Central Library for Students which, since 1923, has carried out similar work in Ireland, with its headquarters in Dublin.

Although much use is made of the facilities for the interlending of books between libraries, the system is by no means fully used. Many who should use it, know nothing of it; many of the smaller libraries lack the bibliographical equipment to enable them to make adequate use of the service. Field work by members of the staff of regional library bureaux is most desirable in order to ensure their more general use, and there is still much that remains to be done by way of local publicity.

CHAPTER XVII

REPORTS AND STATISTICS

THE methods of working of the governing bodies of libraries vary, but a usual feature of each meeting of governors or committee is the submission and consideration of a report by the librarian. At the ordinary meetings, generally, though not always, held at monthly intervals, the report will contain some features which form an invariable part of it, such as statistical tables of the use of the library and its various departments for the period immediately before the meeting, and details of numbers of books added to the stock and their cost, and of future requirements. The routine report, framed in this way, is a great aid to a librarian in keeping his committee in touch with the work being done, and in putting forward any new ideas or schemes, and is a considerable help to the chairman in directing the proceedings.

The most important form of library report is that prepared once a year to review the work of the year immediately past. This can be both a record of achievements and a vehicle for new ideas and, over a series of years, may be the story in serial form of the work of the library to which it applies. Too often, however, annual reports are dull, as they are framed to a regular and unvarying pattern, and with one main object—to demonstrate that the year under review has been the most successful year in the history of the library.

The annual report of a library is best presented in two parts: the first, narrative; the second, statistical. Both should deal with the matter to be presented in broad groups—bookstock, membership, the use made of the service provided, staff, buildings, and finance. Each is an integral part of the system. Larger library systems will add departmental sections to the report. A skilfully written general introduction may be used to summarise the main features of the year's work, which should indicate both successes and failures; and into this introduction may be woven suggestions for future developments, which, if progressive, year by year, can be very effective. It is not given to every one to be able to write well, and the best method to adopt is to say what needs saying as simply and briefly as possible, and without any straining after effect. The main thing is to have something to say that is worth saying.

Following the introduction come the sections of the report, and then, where they are included, the departmental surveys.

The report on bookstock should give the summarised particulars of additions and withdrawals, showing thus the strength of the stock at the beginning and end of the year under review. To this should be added notes on special purchases, on such subject surveys as may have been carried out during the year, on the state of the book market, and the anticipated trend of purchases during the immediate future. Attention should be directed to gifts of books during the year, special reference being made to any gift of unusual importance. If there have been opportunities to acquire desirable additions to the book stock during the year that have had to be foregone through lack of money, this should be pointed out here, though it will call for fuller mention in the section dealing with finance.

The subject of membership will not affect libraries of universities or societies, but is an important part of the affairs of public libraries. The main facts to chronicle are the total membership, and the comparison of this with that of previous years, but variations in practice in libraries produce results which make it difficult to compare membership of the libraries of different authorities. In all, some form of registration is required, but the period for which registration is valid varies from one year to no time limit at all, though the period most usual is two years, an extra three months' grace being allowed for renewal. If records are carefully kept, they show that during each year the number of membership tickets in use at any time is much below the total number of tickets issued. They show, also, that many who leave the neighbourhood do not bring or send in their tickets for cancellation. When comparisons are made, therefore, between library and library, or in the same library for different years, the effective standard of comparison is the number of membership tickets in actual use, and not the number issued and available for use, according to the practice of the library concerned. In the report both figures should be given, if possible, with any relevant comparisons.

The section of the report dealing with the use made of the library, usually called 'issues of books,' should be partly narrative and partly statistical. The trends of reading should be reviewed, and details may usefully be given of the books that have been in greatest demand through the year. These will generally be recently published books, though sometimes older books experience a revival of interest, e.g. through the making of a film version of a novel or of a biography. Most libraries have a system of reserving or bespeaking books specially required by members, a system often confined to non-fiction, and details of the use made of this service should be included here. The statistical table should be arranged so that it shows the number of books issued in each of the main branches of knowledge, as divided by the scheme of classification in use, in each of the departments of the central library and in each of the branch libraries. Comparative figures for the previous year should be added by way of comment to show increases or decreases. The use made of the national system of interlending of books should be dealt with here.

The report on staff is often limited to a statement of examination successes during the year, but sometimes all changes in staff are recorded. Any special staff services should be noted, as for example the work done by many library staffs during the war in paper salvage drives. Other activities that call for mention are lectures given by members of the staff to outside bodies, or the arranging by them of special exhibitions.

The subject of buildings increases in importance with the number comprised in the system. In one-building systems, probably a mention of any special feature concerned with the building during the year, such as redecoration, may be all that is necessary; but in systems with half a dozen or more buildings this will not be enough. Attention to buildings must be systematic and planned, and the assistance of the Architectural Department of the authority (whether this be a separate department or, as is more often the case, a sub-department of the Borough or City Surveyor or Engineer) should be sought. First, there should be a systematic scheme of painting and decoration of buildings, inside and out, and a suitable plan for most towns is that this should be done at five-yearly intervals, though local circumstances—industries, types of buildings and others—may render desirable a different interval, longer or shorter. The advantages of such a scheme are obvious: the annual expenditure on this work can be regularised, and the buildings always look well cared for. The assistance of the architect is required for this, but a more important service he can render is to carry out a survey of buildings yearly, and draw up a schedule of items likely to need attention during the coming year—plastering of walls or ceilings, plumbing, tiling and slating, pointing of walls, and other things that declare themselves to the expert eye. The annual report may well include a section dealing with these matters as they have affected the work of the libraries during the preceding year, such as any curtailment of services at one point, and the arrangements made to overcome inconvenience to readers. There will also come in this section of the report an account of any projected developments, e.g. acquisition of sites for new branch libraries or progress in building them.

The report on finance for the year will be mainly in the form of tables of income and expenditure, but when desirable, a narrative report should be added to explain special details or circumstances, those concerned, for example, with shifting values. During the past few years the book market has changed, and the cost price of books has steadily increased, which, in all libraries, has created the need for a higher expenditure on books to maintain an even level of book provision; and to this has been added greater use of most libraries which has also added to the cost for wear and tear, and the cost of upkeep. These are matters which should not be left to explain themselves, and the larger book fund required is more likely to be forthcoming when the reasons for it have been fully explained.

Other financial matters which may well be touched on are contributions to the funds received from other council departments—in towns, that from the Education Committee for school libraries (though such contributions in counties do not call for special mention, as the library committee is a sub-committee of the Education Committee), or from the Public Health Committee for hospital library services. Any donations of money by gift or bequest would also call for mention, though these are few and far between in British libraries; and when, as is hoped, new library legislation makes the service a compulsory one, and supported partly from government grants, as is the education service, the working of this will be a suitable matter for report.

In the larger library systems, with heads of departments who are qualified librarians, it is sometimes the custom to follow the American practice of presenting separate departmental reports, each written and signed by the head of the department concerned. Such departmental reports would come from, e.g., the Reference Librarian, the Librarian of the Central Lending Library, the Superintendent of Branch Libraries, the Children's Librarian, the Schools Librarian, the Librarian of the Commercial Library, of the Music Library, and of any other special departments, such as the Cataloguing Department. These special reports are particularly useful in bringing out the day-to-day preoccupations of the departments, and make interesting comparison with the overall survey which they follow.

The use of statistics in library practice, as in other things, is designed to present in clear and precise fashion the nature and extent of transactions and costs that are capable of being reduced to figures. Accordingly, library statistics deal with the four main divisions of library administration—stock, membership, book issues and finance—and they are usually massed into statistical tables. These may, on the one hand, be presented in summarised form, which first states in words each part of the service and is followed by the total figure or sum of money which applies to that part; and on the other hand, may be presented in the form of graphs or of that form of symbolical diagram which has been used with good effect in documentary films—isotypes.

The statistical tables relating to book stock are arranged in headed columns of subject matter with one line to each of the library departments or services. This shows in easily apprehended form the precise nature of the stock of each unit, and also the total strength of the service in each subject class. If thought desirable, the subject classes can be divided into sections, and in this way, given sufficient detail, not only may the divisional and total stock of books in, e.g., the natural sciences, be given, but also the stock of the subdivisions of that class—chemistry, physics, biology, etc.

The tables of membership should be arranged so as to show the use made of each library in the system, and also the geographical distribution of the membership, which is best shown by using the voting divisions of ward or area. This latter statistical analysis brings to light deficiencies in library coverage, and when considered alongside population tables for the areas concerned, shows up any needs that may exist for new service points.

In this connection it is important to emphasise the need for choosing carefully the sites of service points, which should always be in or very near points to which people are drawn for other purposes—shopping, entertainment, etc. Badly sited service points are wasteful and inefficient, as they do not attract the maximum use of which they are capable; and, in addition, care is needed in deciding the size of unit of service, whether the library is to be one of 5,000 or 25,000 books capacity. Some prefer the smaller and more numerous service points, others the larger, fewer, but more comprehensive. The survey which accompanies the statistical tables of membership may usefully deal with points of this kind.

The statistics of book issues, as already mentioned, will cover both totals and types, and a useful addition is an occasional analysis of one particular feature—either the use of books in a selected area or on a selected subject.

The financial tables of income and expenditure are usually prepared by the treasurer of the authority, and it is customary, though of doubtful advantage, to divide expenditure into two parts, the first dealing with fabric charges, i.e. rents, repayment of loans, rates, taxes and insurance; the second dealing with service charges—books, staff, cleaning and maintenance, office charges and administration generally. The income figures comprise the block vote (from rates in town and county public libraries, or from general funds in universities or special libraries), and a miscellany of usually small items—fines for overdue books, sale of guides or catalogues, grants from other bodies such as public trusts, etc. The number of headings in different reports varies. Some show expenditure in great detail and apportioned to each of the service points; others do not segregate the service points, but use only broad group headings for each main item such as books or staff salaries. The greater detail may lead to increased efficiency, as it shows up at once any disparities of spending in units of approximately equal size; but whether this is shown in annual reports or not, it should be a part of the work of administration.

It is to be regretted that there is no accepted standard for compiling library statistics, as its absence allows much variety of procedure, and renders comparisons between the apparently like figures of one place and those of another of doubtful value. One library listing its issues of books from the reference department may include every reading of a periodical, either checked or estimated; another may not include any figures for this service at all. Some libraries in calculating the book issue figures of lending departments add each day, to the day's total, all books which have been on loan fifteen days, when the period of loan is fourteen days. One library counts every item, whether a leaflet of four pages or a book of four hundred pages, as a book; others ignore pamphlets with fewer than twenty-four or forty-eight pages. It is desirable that these variations of procedure should end, and the way to bring this about is for the Library Association to formulate a set of rules to be used by all libraries in presenting statistics.

Comparison of library service with library service by contrasting published statistics is an interesting and profitable proceeding so long as it is kept within proper bounds. It can lead to healthy competition; it can show to an administrative librarian where his own service appears to be inferior in quality or quantity to that of another authority of comparable size. But before such comparisons can be used to their fullest possible effect, there must be developed an acceptable and accepted method of statistical computation. Statistics should not be used in an attempt to show how much better the service of one authority is than that of another.

Attempts are made from time to time to formulate acceptable standards of use or of expenditure—so much per head of population to be expended on books or staff; so many book issues per head of population to be the optimum to be sought. These suggested standards can be good servants, but are bad masters. It can be shown quite easily that expenditure below a certain level cannot produce a satisfactory service, and that use of a library that falls below a certain level means probably inefficiency of some kind; but beyond this it is not desirable to go.

CHAPTER XVIII

PUBLICITY

THOSE who have formed the habit of reading when young, and have been familiar with libraries and the services they perform from their schooldays, should need no incentive to use them. For most of us reading is the only way by which we can keep abreast of the times, or find means to follow mental interests and personal tastes, though it is nowadays ably accompanied by broadcasting. With broadcasting, however, the listener must take what is offered; there is no such limit to the reader.

It is fortunate that the number of readers should be so considerable, because reading is the broad highway to education, and for the sake of the welfare both of the individual and of the nation as a whole, it is most desirable that every educational method should be developed as widely as possible. Individuals, if they are to play their proper part in the democratic way of life, must have sufficient learning to enable them to criticise and judge the programmes of government submitted to their decision; and, if they are to live a full life, the arts and sciences should be brought much more widely into human associations than they have ever before been. The greatest enemy of human progress is personal ignorance.

Herein lies the need for good libraries everywhere, but to those who know their work intimately, particularly that of the public libraries, it is very evident that, great as is the use made of them, it is not as great as it should be. Many do not know or use the service provided for them; and the quality of much of the use that is made of them could well be improved.

These are the two aspects of library work which require publicity: first, to make libraries and their work more widely known and used; secondly, to improve the quality of the use made of them.

A first requirement is the improvement of the library service as a whole. Many towns and counties provide an excellent service, but in many it is wretchedly inefficient. The reasons for inefficiency, where it exists, have been thoroughly studied; and plans have been devised for general improvement, many of which are stated or implied in the post-war proposals of the Library Association. It would be fatuous to publicise an inefficient service, as those attracted to it by advertisement or otherwise would quickly perceive its weakness, and not be slow to deride it. The first essential, therefore, is the levelling up of the library service as a whole to an agreed minimum of provision and performance, while in no way interfering with libraries providing a service above the minimum standard laid down. How to accomplish this has been the subject of much discussion and conference, and it appears to be agreed generally that desirable change can only be brought about through government intervention by Act of Parliament, and the subsidising of local expenditure from the national exchequer by a system of grants in aid similar to those made in connection with compulsory education. Other changes, possibly some changes in area of administration, also appear to be required, though this is a very controversial point.

Publicity matters in connection with library service at the present time cannot usefully be made national in scope beyond the limits of requiring the establishment of a minimum standard everywhere, and whatever may be done in this direction will be a fitting task for the Library Association, which is being pressed from many directions to appoint a public relations officer and to conduct national publicity. It would be a task similar in many ways to that carried out by the Carnegie United Kingdom Trust in the 1920's, which was so successful in obtaining the approval of county councils for the establishment of county libraries; but in many respects the task should now be easier, because the work of libraries has grown considerably since 1920, and thousands who before that date made no use of the public library service, often because none was available, now use it regularly. National publicity should begin by pointing out the poverty of many services, often due to the low rateable value of the places concerned, and the need for new legislation to overcome this fundamental difficulty. It might, at the same time, draw attention to the work of the National Central Library and the Regional Library Bureaux, and the service they are doing in arranging the interlending of books between libraries for the benefit of readers all over the country.

Local publicity need not in any way clash with national publicity; indeed, the two should be complementary to each other; but, as already pointed out, a prerequisite of local publicity is the existence of a good service that makes no claim to being able to do what, in fact, it cannot do. To distribute posters and handbills saying, "The Public Library exists for the Public Service," without being able to produce what the public ask for is stupid; and equally stupid it is to make widespread claims such as, "You want the best books—we have them," unless it is quite certain that such is the case.

Effective publicity is not to be found in such crudities, though posters, suitably worded, may be used with good effect. Other methods include the use of the press, leaflets, bulletins or magazines, displays, exhibitions and, in the larger libraries, conducted tours. Each of these has its own place, and the able publicist will use all of them.

Posters may be used alone or as an integrated part of book displays. Used alone they may draw attention to particular activities—the holding of lectures or discussion groups, the opening of a new library or department or activity—a new branch library, for example, or a special department devoted to the fine arts, or a gramophone club. Where posters of this kind are used, they should be designed by a poster artist, and not left to the casual attention of a jobbing printer; what is possible in this respect has been ably demonstrated by the Central Office of Information and the Arts Council.

Local newspapers are probably the best means of publicity for libraries, and most of them are very ready to help. Editors know that many of their readers use the libraries and are interested in any new developments, which are treated as local news, e.g. gifts to the library, exhibitions being held, notable purchases, unusual enquiries answered, and often, when information, particularly on local historical matters, is supplied to the newspaper for its own purposes, acknowledgment of this is given.

Leaflets are produced by libraries in great variety, and a national effort of this kind is now conducted by the Library Association through its Publications Committee. The great advantage of the leaflet is that it is small in size and easily comprehended, and its chief requirements are that it should deal with its subject in a way likely to attract the immediate interest of all who handle it, and that it should be good typographically. Many libraries use this form of publicity to draw attention to recent additions to the stock; others to bring to notice interesting books which appear to have missed the attention they deserve; others again to link the bookstock to local or national events. The artist in typography can render good service here by giving advice on type to be used and general layout.

An extended form of publicity of the leaflet type is the publication of a periodical library journal or bulletin; and as to the production of these, the same need for good style of printing and general layout applies as with leaflets. Bulletins vary in kind. Some consist entirely of classified lists of additions to the library; others combine this with short articles, either topical or local in subject; some deal only incidentally with additions to the library, but give much space to special subject matter concerned with the bookstock, either in narrative or bibliographical form. They vary greatly in size, also, from small pamphlets of a dozen pages to quartos of a hundred or more pages.

Forms of publicity outlined to this point are mainly concerned with print, but exhibitions and personal visits of members of the staff to give talks on the work of the library are equally valuable. Exhibitions may be held either in the libraries or elsewhere, as at conferences or conventions. They require, in all cases, very special care in their composition and mounting. It is a feature of many of the recently built libraries to have display windows either facing the street as shop windows do, or in the entrance hall. These display windows and well designed cases can be used with good effect to draw attention to a changing series of books. The layout is important, and use should be made of stands and steps and of carefully fitted strip lighting. The technique so well developed in many museums may be studied with much profit by all who are considering this method of publicity, as may that of many of the larger general stores. In arranging the material of such exhibitions, a very important feature is the labelling of the objects comprised in them. Hand lettering is best, but this should be attempted only by those who are properly instructed in the art of lettering. A special form of typewriter, which types block capitals about four times as large as the ordinary typewriter letters, is used in some libraries and museums. In addition to the small labels describing the different objects, it is sometimes possible to add showcards giving general information in connection with the exhibition, and good use can be made in these of carefully contrasted colours of ink and water-colour.

Exhibitions outside the library are sometimes held at general exhibitions in town or village, such as gardening exhibitions, or those organised as part of annual conferences of various bodies. In this case, it is better to plan the library display in relation to the general subject matter of the larger exhibition of which it is to form a part, rather than to have a stereotyped library exhibition of general interest.

Conducted tours of the library and its various departments are a most useful method of introducing the service. In some towns, a regular practice is made of bringing parties of boys and girls about to leave school to be shown round the library, and to have the various parts—the classification scheme, the catalogue, the reference library, etc.—described to them by a member of the staff. Occasionally a local society will ask for a similar demonstration, and all applications of this kind should be welcomed.

Invitations are often received by librarians from local societies and clubs to address the members on the contents and use of the library, or on some literary topic. This is useful work, but it should be shared by the whole of the senior staff.

But the best publicity of all is the building up and maintaining of a high standard of public service to all who come to the library and make use of it. Often this is taken for granted, and the staff are left in ignorance whether their services have been appreciated or not; but occasionally letters of commendation come, and these, equally with complaints when they are made, should be passed on to the persons concerned. If the service is alive to all opportunities that may present themselves, comment will surely come, good and bad; if there is no expression of opinion to be heard, there is good reason to suspect the apathy which comes from indifference. When library service touches the lives of people in any significant way, they are sure to talk about it to their friends and associates, many of whom will in turn test its value to their own problems or questions. And the work of a well-managed library can touch a great variety of interests—the business firm with a need for information on some trading point concerned with home or foreign markets, or of a piece of translation from a foreign language, or the address of another business firm; the historical society with a map or manuscript that needs fitting into its context or environment; the scientific society that needs publicity for its meetings or a home for its archives; the research worker with a project connected with the industrial or historical development of the locality. These, and many other opportunities for service present themselves, and their satisfactory treatment is sure of mention and will lead to other opportunities.

Publicity in libraries, then, is both special and general: special, as directed to the advertisement of different services and resources, mainly by printed poster, bulletin or leaflet; general, in that all the services of all the departments are public services which will be open to discussion, comment and criticism. It is important because of its potential effect on the attitude generally adopted towards the local library, which, in turn, will influence the support it receives both for upkeep and work. In all the plans that may be adopted, the highest possible standard should be set, and the co-operation of the whole of the staff should be ensured. Plans should be preceded by discussion, and ideas, whether adopted or not, and from wherever they may be received, should be fully and carefully considered. Most library staffs have one or two members who have special talent for display or artistry, and their talent should be utilised. When such talent is not available on the staff—and, indeed, even when it is—the co-operation of the local school of art should be sought, and particularly if there is a school of typography. Some libraries employ commercial artists for special work, and this is likely to become more common. Expenditure in this way is usually money well spent.

Above all, it is better to do little and to do it well than to attempt much and only achieve the bad or even the indifferent.

Particular attention should be given by the student of library publicity to the work of Dr. E. A. Savage, whose book, *A Manual of Book Classification and Display,* has much in it that touches this subject which is both wise and well-tested.

CHAPTER XIX

THE LIBRARY ASSOCIATION

THE Library Association is a professional association with a royal charter, which gives it some legal privileges (including perpetual succession, and the monopoly of certain matters connected with the profession of librarianship as practised in the British Isles), and lays on it certain obligations. The royal charter was granted on 17th February, 1898, but the Association came into being as the Library Association of the United Kingdom at an international conference of librarians held in London in October, 1877. The first meeting of its Council or governing body was held in February, 1878. During the twenty years that passed between the formation of the Association and the successful application for a royal charter, at council meetings, general meetings of members and the annual conference, the way was paved for the work and influence of the Association as it is to-day. Committees of the Council were set up to advise on codes of cataloguing rules, on size notation of books, on statistics, and on the training of librarians. The forerunners of the *Library Association Record*—*Monthly Notes*, *The Library Chronicle* and *The Library* —ran their course. The annual conference, an important occasion from the beginning, met at important centres all over the kingdom, including Oxford, Manchester, Edinburgh, Cambridge, Liverpool, Birmingham, Glasgow, Dublin and Nottingham. From 1882, plans were being laid to influence the adoption of a much needed consolidating Act of Parliament, though this was to take ten years to mature; and plans for training of librarians, beginning in 1880, led to the first Library Association examination in 1885, and to the holding of summer schools from 1893 onwards.

The way was thus paved for the status of incorporation, and for the great influence on library affairs in Great Britain which the Association now possesses. The charter itself sets forth the aims and objects of the work of the Association, which include the following:

> To unite all persons engaged or interested in library work, by holding conferences and meetings for the discussion of bibliographical questions and matters affecting libraries or their regulation or management or otherwise;
>
> To promote the better administration of libraries;
>
> To promote whatever may tend to the improvement of the position and the qualifications of librarians;
>
> To watch any legislation affecting public libraries, and to assist in the promotion of such further legislation as may be considered necessary for the regulation and management or extension of public libraries;
>
> To promote and encourage bibliographical study and research;
>
> To collect, collate and publish (in the form of Transactions, Journals or otherwise) information of service or interest to the Fellows and members of the Association, or for the promotion of the objects of the Corporation;
>
> To form, collect and maintain a Library and Museum;
>
> To hold examinations in librarianship and to issue certificates of efficiency;

To do all such lawful things as are incidental or conducive to the attainment of the above objects.

The affairs of the Association are carried out by an elected Council and a salaried staff, working in the usual English method through committees which divide the work into four broad groups:

1. To arrange a forum for the discussion of all matters relating to libraries, their organisation and their administration;
2. To organise the professional education of librarians, their examination and their registration;
3. To institute and influence research on all matters concerned with librarianship;
4. To conduct the general and domestic affairs of the Association.

The first of these objects, to arrange a forum for discussion, is provided for by the Annual Conference, regional and sectional conferences, and meetings of branches and sections. Branches of the Association have been formed in most of the regional areas, e.g. the North Midland Branch, which embraces the counties of Derby, Leicester, Lincoln, Northampton and Nottingham; and sections have also been formed to deal with specialist interests, e.g. the University and Research Section. Branches and Sections meet at intervals during each year to hear addresses and to hold discussions on matters connected with librarianship that are either local or national in scope, and they are financed by the parent body to which, as they desire, they can make representations; and, on the other hand, when the parent body desires to have any matter widely discussed, e.g. its post-war proposals, it requests Branches and Sections to arrange such discussions. A weakness in the organisation is that, though Sections have direct representation on the Council of the Library Association, Branches do not, and many hope that this weakness will be eliminated in the near future.

The second object, to organise professional education, conduct examinations, and keep a register of chartered librarians, is carried out by two standing committees of the Council, the Education Committee and the Membership Committee. The Education Committee plans the syllabus of examinations, appoints examiners and assessors, and deals with questions of exemption, arranges centres for examinations, and decides on any matters connected with syllabus or examinations raised in correspondence with the Secretary. The Education Committee is not directly concerned with teaching, which is carried out by University College, London, by technical colleges and schools, and, through correspondence courses, by the Association of Assistant Librarians. Since 1946, there have been some half-dozen full time schools of librarianship at technical colleges in England and Scotland, teaching mainly for the Registration examination. Other technical colleges conduct evening classes, attended by assistants in full time employment.

One of the conditions of registration, after passing the requisite examinations in librarianship, is service in a library approved by the Library Association, and both registration of librarians and approval of libraries for this purpose are carried out by the Membership Committee.

The third main object of the work of the Association, to institute research projects, is carried out by the Association's Research Committee. Its work at the present time might suitably include enquiries into the use of microfilm in library work, or on decay and preservation of leather used in bookbinding, or on the compilation and use of statistics. There is no limit to its field of activities, and there needs to be close association between this work and the enquiry department of the Association—a branch of the Association's own library work.

General and domestic affairs centre in the officers of the Association and the work of the Secretary and the salaried staff. They include the voluminous correspondence with members and others, the office preparation for meetings of Council and committees, for conferences, examinations, and a multitude of miscellaneous affairs. With a membership of some 5,000, the work of the different departments has become so heavy that the time has arrived to sectionalise it, placing each section under a responsible departmental head, under the general supervision of the Secretary.

The Library Association has advanced from small beginnings and voluntary officers to a complicated organisation with a yearly expenditure of some £25,000. Its influence in library affairs is considerable and increasing. It has done much to improve the status of librarians, which, in turn, has led to great improvements in library work all over the country. It has negotiated an agreement with publishers and booksellers that enables books to be bought by libraries at a discount not allowed to ordinary purchasers. It has advised many library authorities on the development and improvement of their service; and it maintains contact with other bodies interested in the work of librarianship throughout the world. Its own publications are authoritative, and increasing in numbers, and its work as a whole receives the encouragement and support of libraries and librarians generally.

INDEX

Abstracts, 10, 144
Accessioning of books, 66, 72–3
Accounts, 31, 35, 53
Adams, W. G. S., 41–2
Administration, 47–8, 50, 54, 65–6, 167, 181–2
Almanacs, 58, 141, 149
Alphabetical-classed catalogue, 89–90
Anglo-American code, 88–92
Annual reports, 36, 161–70
Art galleries, 28–9, 125
Artizans' libraries, 38
Arts Council, 174
ASLIB, 144
Association of Assistant Librarians, 183
Association of University Teachers, 156

Bibliographies and bibliography, 22, 59, 68, 83, 102 n. 1, 103, 143, 149, 153–4, 181
Binding, 47–8, 54, 62, 67, 98–9, 106–14, 184
Bodleian Library, 88
Book issue cards, 59–61, 75–6, 132–3, 135–8
Book jackets, 101
Book reviews, 68, 71
Book selection, 22, 31, 68–72, 102
Book sizes, 107, 147, 180
Books for youth, 70
Booksellers, 72–3, 184
Bookstock, 9–10, 21–3, 38, 47–8, 50–1, 57–9, 61–5, 68–105, 162, 167, 175
Borough council, 27–36
Branch libraries, 26, 54, 56–7, 64–5, 68, 70, 95–6, 122, 164–8, 174
British Museum, 16, 27, 88, 90 n. 1, 112

Broadsides, 9, 11
Brown, James Duff, 10, 80, 135
Budgets, 32–3, 35–6, 47–53
Buildings: upkeep, 32, 47–50, 164–5
Bulletins, 94, 174–5
Bye-laws, 124–30

Card catalogue, 90, 94
Care of bookstock, 97–105
Carnegie United Kingdom Trust, 37, 39, 41–4, 115, 152–5, 157, 159–60, 173
Catalogues and cataloguing, 13–16, 43, 54, 57–60, 63–4, 68, 83, 87–96, 147, 166, 168, 180
Census of books, 105
Census of readers, 121–2
Central cataloguing, 95
Central libraries, 17, 19, 26, 57, 64, 70, 95–6, 164
Central Office of Information, 174
Centralised cataloguing, 95–6
Chairman of committee, 34, 161
Chamber of Commerce, 62
Charging methods, 17, 55, 59–61, 131–40
Chaucer House, 154
Chief librarian, 35–6, 49, 68, 72
Children's libraries, 54, 56, 61, 117, 134, 166
Cinema films, 63
Class marks, 75–6, 78–9, 81–4, 93
Classification, 10–11, 57, 61, 64, 78–86, 93, 147–8
Classification décimale, 10
Classified catalogue, 89–90, 93
Cleaning, 47–8, 100
Clerk to committee, 33–5
Collating books, 74, 76

College libraries, 16, 103–4, 115, 156
Colon class system, 10
Commercial libraries, 54, 57, 62, 144–5, 166
Community centres, 31
Conducted tours, 174, 177
Conferences, 45, 175–6, 180–2, 184
Co-operation, 43, 150–60
Co-opted committee members, 30–1
Cotgreave indicator, 55, 130–1
Counters, 55, 59–60, 133–6
County borough council, 27–36
County councils, 27–36, 38, 173
County libraries, 17, 19, 20, 26, 27–36, 39, 42, 63–4, 69–70, 122, 152–3, 157, 168, 173
Cumulative book index, 68
Cutter, C. A., 80, 88
Cuttings, 62, 145

Decimal classification, 10, 80, 82–6
Delegation of powers, 30, 35
Departmental Committee on public libraries 37, 43–4, 128, 144
Departments of library, 54–67, 164, 166–7
Dewey classification, 10, 80, 82–6
Dickman card charging system, 133
Dictionaries, 58, 83, 141–3, 145
Dictionary catalogue, 88–90
Director of education, 33–4
Directories, 58, 128, 145
Display, 20, 24–5, 101–2, 174
Donations, 142, 162, 166, 174
Drama libraries, 54, 62–3
Drama societies, 32

Education Acts, 29, 38–9, 41
Education committee, 28–31, 35, 61–2, 65, 166
Education of librarians, 42–3, 180–3

Educational reading, 21, 46, 57, 65, 170
Edwards, Edward. *Memoirs of libraries*, 37
Enclosures, 55, 59–60, 134
Encyclopædias, 58, 83, 141, 148–9
English catalogue of books, 68
Enquiries, 25, 148–50, 174, 177–8
Equipment and furniture, 47–8, 50, 55, 58–61, 100, 125, 127, 133–6, 138
Estimates, 32–3, 35–6, 47–53
Exhibitions, 31, 65, 164, 174–6

Faculty libraries, 16
Fiction, 21, 25, 69–70, 86, 88
Films, 63
Finance, 29, 32–3, 35–6, 47–53, 157–9, 162, 165–9
Finance committee, 33, 49
Fines, 52–3, 97, 126–7, 138–40, 168
Further education, 54, 65, 137, 153

Government grants, 40–1, 45, 62, 65, 118, 122, 154, 159, 166, 172
Government publications, 144
Gramophone records, 9, 63, 102
Guarantors, 117, 121–2, 127, 139

H.M.S.O. publications, 144
Haines, H. *Living with books*, 68
Hansard, 144
Henry Watson Music Library, 63
Historical MSS. Commission, 144
Hospital libraries, 166
Huxley's definition of classification, 80–1

Indicators, 55, 130–1
Inspection of libraries, 40, 45

Institut International de Bibliographie, 10
Inter-library loans, 26, 43, 50, 115, 137–8, 151–60, 164, 173
Interchangeability of tickets, 43, 117–18
Ireland, 29, 37, 41, 160
Issues, 16–17, 55, 58–61, 131–40, 163–4, 168–70

Jevons, W. S. *Works on logic*, 80
Joint Standing Committee on Library Co-operation, 156

Kelly, Grace, 148

Labels, 75, 136–7
Lantern slides, 9, 63, 102, 119
Leaflets, 174–5
Lectures, 31, 63, 65, 164, 174
Lending libraries, 54–61, 87, 96, 102–5, 127–8, 131–40, 166, 169
Libraries Offences Act, 125
Library, 180
Library areas, 44–5, 172
Library Association, 180–4, *et passim*
Library authority, 27–36, 38–9, 47, 49, 124–5
Library chronicle, 180
Library committee, 27–36, 72, 161
Library departments, 54–67
Library of Congress, 10, 80, 95, 147
Literary societies, 32
Loans, 29, 47–8
Local committees, 36
Local history, 58, 70, 147, 149, 174
London and Home Counties Branch of Library Association, 128
London School of Economics, 90 n. 1

McColvin, L. R. *Library stock*, 68
McColvin Report, 37, 44, 122
Mansbridge, Dr. A., 151
Manuscripts, 9, 66, 126, 149–50
Maps, 9, 101–2, 126, 130
Mechanical charging, 17, 60–1, 133
Mechanics' institutes, 38
Membership, 31, 115–23, 127, 129, 163, 167
Metropolitan public libraries, 43, 118, 154
Microfilms, 9, 66, 119, 149–50, 183
Ministry of Education, 62, 65, 122
Minto, J. *Reference books*, 143
Mitchell, J. M., 42
Monthly notes, 180
Mudge, I. *Guide to reference books*, 143
Munford, W. A. *Basic stock*, 70
Museums, 28–9, 125
Music libraries, 54, 62–3, 166

National Book League, 22
National Central Library, 43, 115, 137, 151–9, 173
National libraries, 16, 20, 27
Negatives, 102
Net book agreement, 72, 184
New libraries, 47, 68–70, 165, 174
Newspapers, 113, 126, 145, 174
Non-fiction, 21–3, 58, 69–70, 88, 152, 164
North Midland Branch of Library Association, 182

Offences, 125–30
Outlier libraries, 115, 152–4
Overdue books, 121, 126, 138–40, 157, 168

Pamphlets, 9, 126, 147, 169
Parks, 28–9

INDEX

Parliamentary debates, 144
Periodicals, 9–10, 48, 56, 62, 68, 71, 83, 126, 128, 144–5, 169
Photographic department, 54, 57, 66
Photographs, 126, 147, 149
Photostat, 149
Pianos, 63
Pictures, 9, 11, 63, 101–2, 119, 126, 147
Plan cases, 102, 147
Planning, 55–60
Play sets, 63, 119–20
Pool-stock, 62, 64, 70
Posters, 173–4
Printing, 48, 90, 94–6, 174–5
Prints, 9, 11, 63, 101–2, 119, 126, 147
Processing of books, 74–7
Public health committee, 166
Public Libraries Acts, 28–9, 37–41, 43, 115–16, 118, 124–6, 140, 159, 172, 180–1
Public library systems, 37–46
Publicity, 20, 54, 67, 94, 171–9
Punched card system, 60–1, 133

Ranganathan, S. R., 10
Rates, 29, 33, 38–42, 45, 48, 52, 168
Readability, 69
Readers, 16–21, 24–5, 69, 71, 115–23, 127, 129, 163, 167
Readers' adviser, 17, 25
Readers' tickets, 59–61, 117–23, 127, 132–3, 136–7, 163
Reading lists, 24, 94, 174–5, 178
Reading rooms, 56, 126
Receipts, 52–3
Recreational reading, 21, 25, 46, 69
Reference libraries, 16, 43–4, 54, 56–9, 62, 66, 88, 98, 101, 102 n. 1, 103, 112, 119, 122, 126, 128, 141–50, 166, 169
Regional library bureaux, 26, 43, 50, 137–8, 154–60, 173

Regional reference libraries, 44
Registration of librarians, 182–3
Registration of readers, 118–23, 129, 163
Regulations, 20, 97, 116, 124–30
Repair of books, 62, 99–101, 113
Reports, 35–6, 161–70
Research libraries, 10–11, 27
Reservation of books, 128, 164
Reserve stock, 87–8, 102–3, 146
Revision of bookstock, 22–3, 69–71, 102–3
Rockefeller Trust, 44
Routine, 9–18
Royal Commission reports, 144
Rural community associations, 31–2

Salaries and wages, 47–8, 50, 52
Savage, Dr. E. A., 147–8, 179
Sayers, W. C. Berwick, 81
School libraries, 54, 61–2, 166
Scotland, 29, 37, 40–1, 125–6, 159
Separates, 9
Serials, 9, 143–4
Sheaf catalogue, 90–1
Shelf arrangement, 10–12, 61, 75, 78–9, 97, 99–100, 147
Shelf register, 104
Shelving, 55, 59, 61–2, 146
Society publications, 91, 143–4
Solander cases, 101
Sound-proof rooms, 63
Special libraries, 10–11, 17, 20, 27, 47, 50, 152–3, 168
Stacks, 146
Staff, 48, 50, 52, 60–1, 67–8, 71, 126, 128–9, 146, 148, 164, 175, 177–8, 181
Stamps and stamping, 74, 76, 137
Standards of service, 40–1, 44–6, 118, 170, 172–3, 177–9
Statistics, 161–70, 180, 184

INDEX 189

Stock cards, 71-2, 104-5
Stocktaking, 103-5
Stores department, 54, 66
Subject classification, 10, 80
Subject grouping, 147-8
Subject index to periodicals, 83
Subscription members, 116, 122
Summer schools, 181
Superannuation, 48
Survey of buildings, 32, 49-50, 164-5
Surveys of libraries, 37, 41-2

Technical libraries, 54, 57, 62
Tenders, 32
Time-tables, 141
Town clerk, 33-4
Trade-catalogues, 62, 92, 145
Turntables, 60, 138
Tutorial classes, 65, 137, 153

Union catalogues, 43, 96, 154-7
University and Research Section of Library Association, 182

University College, London, 183
University libraries, 16-17, 20, 27, 50, 103-4, 115, 156, 168
Urban district council, 27-36

Vertical files, 101, 147
Village centres, 17, 19, 26, 64
Visual aids, 54, 63

Wellard, J. H. *Book selection,* 68
Whitaker's cumulative book list, 68
Wicket gates, 60, 136
Withdrawals, 22, 71, 102-3, 162
Workers' Educational Association, 65, 151

Yearbooks, 141
Yorkshire regional system, 156

For Product Safety Concerns and Information please contact our EU
representative GPSR@taylorandfrancis.com
Taylor & Francis Verlag GmbH, Kaufingerstraße 24, 80331 München, Germany

www.ingramcontent.com/pod-product-compliance
Lightning Source LLC
Chambersburg PA
CBHW061835300426
44115CB00013B/2388